WORMS
ON
PARACHUTES

Mystical Allies In My Cancer Survival

By

Sarah-Jane Phillips

First published in 2013 by Sarah-Jane Phillips

ISBN 978-1482058116

Printed by Amazon's Createspace

Typeset by Ramesh Kumar Pitchai
Front/Back cover design by Angie Joint
Front cover illustration by Annabel Phillips.

Reviews:

Was lucky enough to read Worms on Parachutes as Sarah was finalising it! As an oncologist I have been on this journey with many patients, but it was still so eye-opening to read such a candid and well-written story. Sarah's journey and spirit are incredible. Maybe it isn't meant to be but for an American healthcare employee like myself it is also wonderful story of a healthcare system that works, that takes care of people. And it is a sweet love story – Sarah's devoted husband is beautifully captured as the loving man in her life who wants to help even if he doesn't always know how. A Beautiful book.

Wendy Woodward

This book should be published. It's too important a book to be missed by the hundreds of thousands of families touched by cancer every year. Sarah's writing is from the heart. Sarah shows us what strength is. Readers of this book will derive strength from it and will be inspired to fight just as hard. I am truly honoured to be writing the foreword for this book, and overwhelmed by the task of making it worthy of such a well told amazing story. Sarah is the definition of a survivor

Richard Amos

Worms on Parachutes is a book for everyone. I have been lucky enough to read it already. It is the most fantastic account of Sarah's battle against Cancer, not once but twice in her life!!! The uplifting story is told with Sarah's complete honesty and shows how the love and support of her family, friends and medical team have helped her through. You really must read it. The section on Worms on Parachutes is fascinating!! This book is not just for those with breast cancer although there is no doubt it will help others touched by it, but this book is for everyone: anyone who wants to laugh, to cry or simply be inspired by one amazing beautiful lady. I will remember this book forever!! Please Note: tissues are required for the reading of this book!!

Laura Carter-Browne

Worms on Parachutes is a story of success and bravery through terrible adversity. Whilst it deals with struggles and familial issues as a result, during very scary and painful times, the reader is reminded throughout of the power of positive thinking. I won't lie, it's a tear-jerker, but by the end you feel that even in reality, the good guys can and DO win. The story is not about the outcome, but about the experience Sarah went through, and how she has changed as a result. It is an inspiring and moving personal journey fighting against a disease that sadly affects most of us, directly or indirectly. Many will want to read about the indomitable human spirit's struggle against survival and what that teaches us.

Aurora Harley

For

Giles,

Olivia Jane and Annabel Louise

With all my heart

Worms on Parachutes - Mystical allies in my cancer survival.

Sarah-Jane Phillips has made her home in a village in Bedfordshire, in the English Home Counties, north of London, where she lives with her husband and two daughters. After surviving two forms of cancer, the latter being breast cancer, she decided to finally find the courage to write her very personal journey on her relationship with the disease in the hope of inspiring others faced with a similar traumatic set back.

For more information on Sarah please follow her on Twitter@Sarahwop19 or find her on Facebook on Sarah's Worms on Parachutes page.

Proceeds of the sales of the book will go towards the National Health Service as a token of appreciation for the exceptional care received.

Contents

Foreword

What lies behind us and what lies before
us are tiny matters compared to what lies
within us

-Ralph Waldo Emerson.

Cancer is a word that continues to instil fear into all of us. So many countless families around the world are impacted by cancer every year that it is difficult to find someone whose family has not been touched by the disease. Yet, so many stories of survivorship remain untold.

As a professional with sixteen years experience in radiotherapy I have interacted with numerous cancer patients during their battle with the disease. As a parent, however, the patients that impact me the most on an emotional level are children and young mothers. Sarah's story describes her battles with cancer both as a child, and later as a young mother.

I first met Sarah in the mid 1980's when we were teenagers. Her family had returned to England after years of living overseas and temporarily settled near my hometown in Shropshire. Sarah was instantly popular at school. She was attractive, funny, friendly, intelligent, and seemed to have an experience of the world that transcended our small town. Her love for life was infectious, and she portrayed herself with a confidence I had rarely seen at that point in my life. It was already clear in those days that Sarah was a very special person. It was clear that Sarah would rise to meet any challenge, seemingly with ease, and would have a positive effect on everyone she interacted with.

Sarah's family didn't stay long in Shropshire before relocating to Hertfordshire. One day, I received a letter from Sarah. The tone of her letter was characteristically upbeat as it went on to explain how she had been diagnosed with Hodgkin's lymphoma. The letter continued to briefly describe that Sarah had been through radiotherapy, and that she was now feeling fine. Enclosed with the letter were a couple of photographs of Sarah taken on a family holiday after her treatment had finished, and she looked great. I was stunned to learn that a friend of mine had had cancer, and I could not comprehend that such a thing could happen to a young, healthy teenager. However, Sarah's unshakeable positive attitude was so clearly communicated through her words that her letter did nothing to help me truly appreciate the battle that she, and her family, had just fought.

As is the case with almost all of us, life moves on, we get busy with families and careers, and we lose touch with many childhood friends. Then, of course, through the advent of social media, many of those old contacts are re-established. Reconnecting with Sarah I was delighted to learn that she was doing well, was married, and had started a family. Her zest for life was still as evident as ever, and then, just as she had done before, she casually mentioned that she had recently completed treatment for breast cancer. Not just any breast cancer, but triple negative breast cancer, the most aggressive sub-type of the disease. This time I was not fooled by her nonchalance. I knew that she had been through the fight of her life. I knew that it had been tough. However, I still did not truly appreciate just how tough until I read her incredible story.

I see cancer patients every day of my professional life. I see fear, trepidation, courage, strength, humour. I see compassion and understanding shared between patients, and I see unwavering support from patient's loved ones. Sarah's story allowed me to see these from a very different vantage point. Sarah has told her story with an honesty that draws the reader in and carries them along on her journey as she battles cancer for the second time in her life. It's difficult to not feel the emotional highs and lows of her journey, and to not be awe struck by her courage as she attacked her disease, refusing to let it attack her. Sarah describes beautifully the love and support provided by her husband, Giles, and faith her children had in their mother's will to survive. Her story is also tribute to the commitment of her surgeon as he fights alongside Sarah with just as much relentlessness, and to the National Health Service which is arguably the best healthcare system in the world.

Sarah is as driven and positive today as she was back in Shropshire all those years ago. She is committed to helping others in the fight against breast cancer and has since run the London marathon and conducted media interviews to raise awareness. Sarah is an inspiration to all of us, and her story of survivorship will give hope to those touched by cancer.

Richard A. Amos
Division of Radiation Oncology
The University of Texas MD Anderson Cancer Center
Houston, Texas. USA
October, 2012

Worms on parachutes

Far off, they looked in the hazy altitude like paratroopers filling the skies, canopies opening and tiny figures softly descending. It was like a war film as they landed amidst the poppy fields that were, in truth, my hospital bed-covers.

As they neared the ground I realised they were not soldiers in fatigues. They were happy worms on parachutes, gaudily dressed and wearing large Elton John-style sun-glasses. They landed all over me with the lightness of feathers.

That was how I emerged from my coma to the world. The worms conveyed messages of love and support. Weird though it is, they remain in my imagination, my tiny allies in a war with the killer cells. I hope they never surrender.

1

Looking forward, thinking back

London-Luton Airport. The departures lounge heaves with travellers. I sat with my family, excited about our impending summer holiday and waiting for our flight to be called. I caught myself people watching - airports are perfect for it. Looking and feeling the bustle that afternoon, I pondered: where all the passengers had come from, what journeys had they made and where life would be leading them. Life's journey is for everybody a single destination. But our journeys are also individual. Looking around me I assumed many fellow passengers were fortunate to reach that point travelling every path as they had planned it; they were, in my presumption, in control of their destiny. Life just passes by smoothly, almost without interruption. For the less fortunate, and actually nobody knows why, our bodies are invaded by the enemy; their mission is a physical attack, combined with a psychological battle so we feel control is taken from us, leaving us exposed, vulnerable and terribly frightened. That enemy is called cancer.

I reflected on my experiences. I had just emerged successfully from a battle with breast cancer. It was the second time I had faced the dreaded disease, though in a different form. As travellers milled around, I scanned faces, knowing there must be others among those outwardly self-confident people secretly sharing the desperation I felt when first diagnosed: *this is the end of the world.* That's when I decided to record my experiences, in the hopes of encouraging others who face a similar traumatic set-back.

If they were bothered, the other travellers in the lounge might casually notice me if they, too, were people watching: a mum in her early forties, quite short blonde bobbed hair, surrounded by her most precious assets, her two lovely daughters and her husband, and assume a long awaited, joyous holiday awaited them. They would read appearances: I've mastered the art of disguising my anxieties and the shadow that haunts me. I want to exude determination because I will prevail.

Regaining life and confidence from the grip of a callous disease teaches tough lessons. At the outset, I couldn't help but feel that my body was betraying me again after being struck with breast cancer at the age of thirty six - and cancer for the second time in my life as Hodgkin's disease struck me at sixteen.

Nothing will ever prepare you for a diagnosis of cancer and the initial feelings: fear, a sense of defencelessness, a victim at the mercy of fates. Somehow over the course of time, from deep within, you manage to draw strength and personal significance; will-power takes shape. I hope one day I will be able to reach out and help; to educate others through insights into how I felt at the time of treatment; to relay hope to others beset with an unwelcome intrusion into their lives; and demonstrate how it is possible to emerge stronger, more positive, and realise true priorities.

Despite its critics, the National Health Service (NHS) – especially its surgeons, doctors, paramedical teams, nurses and researchers - is a very special institution to me. It is undervalued by the opinionated elites almost to the extent that it needs a preservation order – yet it is cherished by the public it serves. And, of course, it is the symbol of Britain's welfare for its people. I hope the 'patient' aspect of my experience will be of value; it is part of my motivation. My account is not meant to be a medical text book; it is my own interpretation and understanding of what I experienced at a level of my comprehension.

The last few years have been tumultuous, with both funny and sad occurrences, over-arched by a need to retain a sense of humour – dark and light - at the most inappropriate times! My emotions ran high. Huge fears confronted me as I endured harsh, brutal treatment to rid me of a disease that was threatening to completely shut down my system. In response, I clung to the promise the treatment would allow me to stay close to the people that I truly love. The test of relationships is immense. But equally the growth in trust and support in the face of adversity more than compensates. At a time when I should have been dedicated to bringing up my young family our roles reversed: they, in effect, ended up looking after me and encouraging my recovery. To me, my experience is extraordinary; but, of course, it could also be considered ordinary. Miracles happen in our hospitals every day, if we only take time to realise it – and at the same time confound the critics and cynics. Thousands can relate to my challenges through their own experiences, or those of loved ones, friends, and friends of friends. My past isn't unique. Serious illnesses like cancer can have differing outcomes. This is just mine.

2

Journeys to the unknown

Life is full of twists and turns, they say. I can't help but feel too many of mine have been round bends in long hospital corridors or through doors to functional consulting rooms, dreary waiting rooms, anxious and fraught filled haematology and oncology departments, and clinical radiology departments. At least my first hospital visit was a joyous occasion.

I was born in New Cross Hospital in Wolverhampton on the 19 March 1971 weighing just 4lbs 3oz but soon developed healthily in the wonderful fresh air of Shropshire for the next three years. The next move was more dramatic as my dad was driven by a belief that all journalists were obliged to witness historic events in the making. As a young family we flew out clandestinely to Salisbury, Rhodesia (now Harare, Zimbabwe) where he joined the country's national newspaper, *The Sunday Mail*. This couldn't have been an easy decision to make with a young family but we were as intent as toddlers could be on making the adventurous move as a united team - dad, mum, my older brother

Richard and me. I must have had the patience of a saint then as my mum always tells me now how after flying for nine hours I asked if we had taken off yet!

My dad was reporting on the civil war and political unrest, a stark contrast to *The Birmingham Post* that he had just left behind. He was away quite frequently, although as children we were completely unaware of the serious situation that the country faced. Instead, we lived what could actually be described as quite a privileged life. Richard and I went to a great school and received a well rounded education where respect and discipline was instilled into every pupil from a very early age. The boys were expected to hold the doors open for the girls, and we all had to open the doors for the teachers or older pupils. Whenever a teacher entered the classroom we would all stand as a mark of courtesy and respect and we would sit again only when we were told to be seated.

I made really wonderful friends and I am thrilled that those friends are still part of my life today. It wasn't just us kids that had great friends; mum and dad had a very active social life, too. Many weekends would be spent all getting together and taking advantage of the glorious sunshine and enjoying the great outdoors, spending the days in the pool and finishing off with barbecues - I still find myself calling them a *braai* (braaivleis) until friends look bemused (so why do they use the Australian slang *barbie*) Quite often we would hire a lodge at the lakes where we were in the thick of seeing all the wildlife roaming around in their natural habitat, from giraffes to rhinos and elephants. We always had to be on guard to ensure that the rhinos didn't sneak up on us from behind and they were notorious for doing that. In the evening we would take ourselves close to the waterholes where we would wait for the animals to grace us with their presence as they came down to their water, no doubt relieved that the blazing dry heat of the day was now cooling, and we would just sit and watch them silently and patiently for hours whilst listening to the harmonious chorus of the crickets and cicadas in the background.

3

White coats

From an early age, I've always been so prone to accidents and illness my mum and dad called me calamity's child. For some reason everything just seemed to happen to me. My parents must have lost count of the number of times they received a phone call to say I was in the local casualty department from anything from a sprained ankle (I was always slipping over on highly polished floors) to breaking my leg after being thrown over the bonnet of a car because I failed to stop at a T-junction whilst riding my bike.

One of the more serious consequences happened when a girlfriend invited me to share a family holiday with her parents. They were great friends of my mum and dad – and remain so. Our mums worked together in the cosmetics department of Barbour's, the equivalent of Selfridges in Salisbury city centre (later Harare). My friend and I met in the department store every Saturday morning and, whilst waiting for our mums to finish work, we would annoy the lift attendants, dressed in their pristine starched khaki uniforms complete with satin cummerbunds, employed to press the control buttons whilst softly advising, "lift going up" or "lift going down", with an almost musical rhythm. Their regular audience included two giggling girls who found the repetitive jingle amusing. But it was sufficient to bond a friendship between Suzanne and myself as we weren't school friends. Her family owned a farm just a couple of hours drive outside the capital. For the first couple of days we really enjoyed frolicking around in the swimming pool and enthusiastically jumping on the trampoline, singing and laughing on the swings, but like all children we bored easily and desperately tried to find other activities to entertain us. Very quickly we cooked our own secretive plan. We organised for the horse handlers to saddle up a couple of horses for us so that we could take ourselves out for a ride all around the farmland and completely off the beaten track. It wasn't until afterwards that I realised they were actually wild horses and used to play polo. Therefore we were not allowed to ride them. I was fortunate to have horse riding lessons as a very young girl and could ride as far as walking and trotting went, but Suzanne had never actually ridden before so we organised rather sensibly for one of the horse handlers to walk alongside her holding the reins as she rode. All saddled up and with the sun beating down on our backs, Suzanne's parents believing we were playing nicely together, we set off for our ride around the acreage of farmland. We both felt excited, not plagued with guilt that we were doing something that we shouldn't. We were only eleven. As we headed off and on to the deserted dirt track and well away from the farmhouse, for some reason and I never established why, Suzanne ordered her handler to release the reins so she was free to ride on her own. We were only leisurely walking - it was easy to control the horse, or so she presumed. But within a shot her horse was off and within seconds mine followed. It was natural in the game of polo. That's what they were trained to do. We both bounced uncontrollably in the leather saddles as the horses literally galloped away when I courageously decided that it would be far safer for me to jump off. Well that's what I tell friends anyway, but I think I actually got thrown off. I hit the hot sand of the dirt track with a thud and couldn't move, paralysed with shock. Moments later Suzanne was thrown from her horse, too, and landed rather awkwardly on her arm. The horse boy immediately ran for help and returned with Suzanne's parents. They were shocked at the outcome of our mischievous behaviour and felt quite anxious about telling my parents. They then spent the next two hours driving us back to Harare to receive medical attention. Inevitably, we both ended up on the children's ward at the main hospital in beds next to each other. I had broken a bone at the base of my back and needed to be put in traction to correct it, whilst Suzanne needed an operation to insert pins through her elbow.

Unfortunately the phone calls didn't stop there. A few months later I cycled home from school with my brother.

Careering downhill I managed to hit a huge black and white oil drum which were used whilst carrying out road works, instead of the orange and white cones they use in England. I was thrown over the handle bars and up into the air before I landed head first on to the tarmac and slid down the road on my face. People didn't wear cycle helmets in those days. I was unconscious and out for the count as I was rushed to hospital by ambulance. My parents, I'm sure, were not prepared for that phone call. What they faced on arrival at hospital was their daughter full of all sorts of tubes and wires, critically ill in intensive care. Judging by what I looked like, they really didn't think I was going to make it, and found it hard to believe the doctor when he told them I'd be alright. I was unconscious for five days, partly due to being in an induced coma and when I did eventually come round I honestly didn't know who my family were, and only spoke complete nonsense for days. Under the care of one of the most able neurosurgeons in Southern Africa, I thankfully made a complete recovery. To this day I still do not have any recollection and detailed memory of that accident or of the early recovery days that followed. My face also escaped scar free, fortuitously.

When I was discharged and sufficiently recovered, my mum and dad filled in the graphic details of my 'spaced out' weeks. They were at my bedside all day, in relays. But when they swopped over I swore nobody had been to see me. I even looked evil. My eyes were wild, my hair stiff and streaked with multiple colours of dried vomit.

Everybody was out to get me. I whispered; I didn't want to be overheard by sinister agents plotting around me.

"See that woman?" I'd ask my mum, dragging her to the toilet to appeal for protection. "…she's out to kidnap me."

Everybody was. The reality shamed my suspicions. The shadowy figures threatening me in hospital came out of my injured brain. They were a distorted memory stored during the bike accident. The delusion derived from the help given to me by removal men who were following down the hill. As I lay unconscious, they covered me with blankets from the van to keep me warm and as comfortable as possible. They kept me safe until the ambulance arrived to take me to the Parirenyatwa Hospital. Their act of humanity and caring probably saved my life. I wish I could meet them again, to thank them for their help. Though, I don't think I remember enough Shona language to speak in their first tongue. But I can say with honesty they were all *mushi sterrik.*

Unable to keep away from the hospital and all the staff that were growing accustomed to my little stays with them, my visits didn't end there. I returned a few months later quite seriously ill and a lumbar puncture revealed bacterial meningitis. I had a raging temperature, a horrendous headache, unable to open my eyes as I failed to tolerate any light or sound. Instead I just lay motionless and limp for days. Thankfully after intravenous antibiotics, great care and plenty of rest in hospital I was soon up and back on my feet again and allowed to go home, where I was instructed to rest and take it easy for a couple of weeks. I remember that rest so vividly, as I recall watching my parent's car drive down our long driveway in the mornings to go to work. As soon as I lost sight of it disappearing though the iron gates, I bounced out of bed and got myself washed and dressed so I was ready to go and help my brother and some friends build a den in some woodland near to home. I would run to the hideout as soon as it was safe to do so and I would spend the day carrying bricks and sticks to build the perfect secret hideout. Afterwards I went home and put my pyjamas back on and pretended I had been in them all day when mum and dad returned from work.

I also had my tonsils removed after years of really suffering from tonsillitis which had me laid up in bed for days at a time and my appendix out following numerous bouts of rumbling appendicitis.

Contrary to all the mishaps and my acquaintance with various white coats, we enjoyed our time in Africa and had lived there for ten years when my family made the decision that my brother and I should return to England to continue our education. This coincided, too, with the country failing to find the stability that we desired. The time seemed right to return.

4

The 'happiest days of your life' turn sour

On returning to England we eventually settled in the Chilterns in Hertfordshire about thirty miles north of London, where I attended the local secondary school. I began enjoying some permanence; everything seemed to be going really well for me. Africa would always be dear to me but it was now behind me, the past; in the comfortable and pleasant surroundings of the Chiltern Hills I wasn't bitten by ticks or other tropical *nasties*, and I hadn't fallen off my bike for years. It was now time to begin to focus on my studies and work towards carving a career. As I had travelled quite extensively as a child the travel industry was my natural choice. I thought about the academic subjects that would help to lead me into my ambition. For once it would be a journey with maps. Like all children developing through school, I selected subjects that I thoroughly enjoyed and that absorbed me and others I excelled in. An exciting life lay ahead.

I was your typical industrious pupil at school, I wasn't 'A' grade but I worked hard, always stayed out of trouble and conformed to all the rules of the school – as instilled in Rhodesia and Zimbabwe. So when the summer holidays were drawing to a close I looked forward to the new term ahead of me and felt quite relaxed and unfazed about venturing into my examination years.

Within four months of beginning my coursework I started to feel unwell and not quite right in myself. I was constantly zapped of all my energy. I was drained, lethargic. Coughs and colds really lasted for weeks. I became pale, suffered headaches at the slightest exertion. Typically maths was always upstairs; sitting through every maths class with a banging headache ambushed my concentration. My skin itched. I suffered bouts of sickness. Suddenly, from figuratively skipping to school each day, the walk to school, especially the short climb up Shukers Hill, became an ordeal. Passing the old people's bungalows, I wheezed heavily and deeply. Fate can sometimes not only be cruel but also have a nasty sense of humour. Despite all my symptoms, the family doctor was quite dismissive. Kids at a healthy age aren't supposed to suffer life-threatening illnesses. So I heard easy rationalising: *I was allergic to my dog, or the washing powder, or I had a virus related to glandular fever*. Meanwhile all I wanted to do was sleep. I secretly worried about myself. Contrary to the complacent diagnoses, I knew with increasing conviction I wasn't well. As activists for patients' rights say today, *it's my body; I know how it feels.* Something, just something, felt seriously wrong. I hadn't always felt that way. My school attendance dropped. I was now taking countless days off school, feeling so guilty but so unwell. Even so, I couldn't truly rest; I found no respite from my worries about the importance of my schoolwork. I was desperate. Weary from the symptoms and bereft by the sinister unknown, I lay on my stomach in bed one evening. I felt a lump in my neck. The plot of the TV soap I had been watching – I think it was *Coronation Street* – suddenly didn't matter; the fates of the characters meaningless. I don't know what made me feel for it. I didn't have any discomfort in my neck. Unconsciously, I had just felt the lump. Then, perplexingly, I found it protruded. Maybe because my fears had been rebuffed in the doctor's surgery I waited until the next morning to almost casually mention the lump to my mum. Instinctively, she was concerned. I was back at the surgery within hours. My doctor examined me. Since I was again suffering a virus, he pondered that perhaps all my glands were swollen so much they had merged. Alternatively, he thought I may have gone on to develop glandular fever. Looking back, perhaps it was due to his kindness, as though he didn't want to damn me with the diagnosis of a traumatic, life-threatening illness, in case his opinion came true. He decided on a blood test to confirm the fever. Within two days he telephoned my mum. The hospital haematology department wanted to see me for further investigations. The laboratory had found something. The haematologist wanted to see me the following day.

5

Hodgkin's disease

The specialist was at Stoke Mandeville Hospital in Aylesbury. She examined me thoroughly and asked me questions to assess my general condition. Her questions were on the button. I had all of the symptoms that she described and I actually felt relieved she understood how I felt. She suggested I have a chest X- ray immediately and was adamant that I must return from the department with the films to discuss the finding straight afterwards. The chest X- ray revealed a huge area of shadowing on both sides of my lungs. It was apparent that what was in my chest would be in my neck as well; two days later I had a biopsy on the lump in my neck. Analysis confirmed Hodgkin's disease – a cancer of the lymphatic system which affects white blood cells. It was June; I was sixteen and had almost come to the end of my first year of exam work.

When you are young, cancer doesn't really feature in your thoughts. With the alert raised by the haematologist's questions, I established I did have an uncle, my dad's brother, who had suffered Hodgkin's disease. (In subsequent consultations, this was regarded as a coincidence on the grounds it is not a hereditary form of the disease.) He had died four years before I was diagnosed, after fighting it for many years. Misguidedly my parents actually denied that he had Hodgkin's disease to try and protect me until I had met survivors of the condition but I always knew and just accepted that they clearly didn't feel that it was the appropriate time to tell me.

At home I took myself to my bedroom. As I lay on top of my bed and looked around my room, newly decorated with pink Marks & Spencer wall paper from the Zara collection, I imagined what it would be like for mum and dad to walk into my room and feel the hollow absence of me never being in there again after I'd died and if they would be able to cope. I think it is always worse for the people left behind to try and pick up the pieces. There is a saying that grief is the price you pay for love and that is very true. Although I had all of those depressed and gloomy thoughts I never shared my feelings or confided in anybody. Instead, I carried them on my shoulders and attempted to carry on as normal. When I look back, though, I don't think I ever felt the depth of fear that I felt much later in life. I think my parents, although unaware of my inner thoughts, chose to shield me as much as they could and carried the burden of worries themselves; I was, after all, still a child in their eyes.

Coincidentally, shortly after my diagnosis, I was asked to complete a piece of English coursework at school on the topic of fear. Feeling quite isolated at the time I chose to write a short story on the fear of the unknown, something I was experiencing first hand with so many questions to ask. Those questions are still unanswered today and probably will be for years to come. Many years later, I was given a copy of that piece of writing after it had been forwarded to my main consultant in Oxford, who requested it was kept and filed in my medical records. I was really touched when I was handed it. To think that they had taken the time to read it and then file it and tell me how beautiful they had found my writing. The final sentence on that piece of work read, I was fighting cancer, it wasn't fighting me, and that was what I was like at sixteen.

My disease was diagnosed as Stage Two B - I also had a growth under my arm, meaning the disease was positive in two or more groups of lymph nodes. The B indicated that I experienced the symptoms as well; I needed to have six sessions of chemotherapy. In the past, chemotherapy made patients very sick. Anti sickness drugs were not prescribed as today. I was sick all evening and all night on the days that I had my treatment, followed by horrific violent retching and awful stomach cramps. I didn't dare look in the mirror as I made my way to the bathroom. I could feel that my face would be deformed with being so drugged up. I always needed to spend four days in bed afterwards just to recover.

I had my chemotherapy at Stoke Mandeville Hospital in Buckinghamshire in the haematology department, which worked directly under the instruction of my main professor who was based at the John Radcliffe Hospital in Oxford. At Stoke Mandeville I met a couple of other patients who made a particular impression, among them a young boy who was being treated for leukaemia. For all the treatment that he had been subjected to over the years, he came across as such a live wire and was the one who always joked with the nurses, who always came across so happy and in high spirits, considering his ordeals. He was a couple of years younger than me and was really blown up with all of his treatment. It was devastating when only a few months later he lost his battle and sadly passed away. The other patient was a young woman a couple of years older than me. We actually spent a few days on the ward together having intravenous antibiotics. She, too, had Hodgkin's disease. I remember her as a really striking girl with the most beautiful dark, curly thick long hair. She had refused to have chemotherapy in the initial stages as she feared losing her luscious locks. Her resistance lasted until she realised the terminal consequences this would have for her. We never did lose all of our hair – instead it just became very fine. Apart from our time spent on the ward together we never did keep in touch afterwards. I actually found it very difficult and challenging to build relationships with cancer patients. I always felt that I may be exposed to something that I preferred to remain ignorant to. I had already watched Steven fight and lose his battle and I felt I needed to protect myself from that experience again. I was still so young.

With my chemotherapy complete I had another CT scan and needed to go back to see my consultant at the John Radcliffe Hospital in Oxford to discuss the results. He was delighted that all the shadowing had disappeared; we had watched it dissipate during my treatment. Great news – the best we could all hope for. My consultant, however, was convinced that we needed to act on the side of caution and suggested I go ahead with six weeks of mantle field radiotherapy. I would need to endure this every day to ensure that any stray cells unable to be seen on scans would be destroyed for good. His aim was simply to cure me.

6

Radiotherapy – the double edged sword.

It was the week after my seventeenth birthday that I went to the Churchill Hospital in Oxford to start my radiotherapy treatment. I was admitted on the Monday morning. I would stay until late on Friday morning when I would then return home following my treatment. This routine continued for six gruelling weeks. Still very determined to sit my exams, the first one was scheduled for two days after my final session. From the outset I would arrive at hospital with all my books and folders to revise. A perfect opportunity with no interruptions, I thought. Little did I know of the effects that radiotherapy would have on me. I would sit on my hospital bed, surrounded by all of my folders full of enthusiasm to revise and within ten minutes I would be fast asleep, only to woken by the nurses when it was time to make the walk along the long corridors: the Churchill hospital was a really old military hospital used in the second world war, all on one level, until I reached the radiotherapy unit. I needed a handkerchief smothered in Vicks vapours held over my nose and mouth like a mask to take those walks, just to reduce my strong sense of smell that was becoming so sensitive and heightened. The smell of the hospital linen in the corridors, the food cooking in the kitchen, the smell of the strength of the cleaning disinfectants – all so exaggerated to the point of making me heave and retch as I waddled along the corridors in my hospital gown, eventually throwing up at some point along the way, apologising to the those who came to help me.

Just as a comparison I only had to smell the aroma of the coffee percolator used the previous Sunday still lingering in the air as I put the key in the front door when I returned home on the Friday afternoon and I would be violently sick on the doorstep.

My dad still vividly remembers my determination when he visited hospital before and after work. Just watching me attempt my revision, to then set off for my treatment, to return, throw up in the sink in my room, return to my bed and my textbooks, and then to just fall asleep, only to repeat it all over again the following day. The thought of deferring my exams until the following year, as suggested by my doctors and consultants, was not a serious option for me. I needed to move on with my life. I continued with my studies as much as I could, but eventually came to the conclusion that I needed to concentrate on my strongest subjects that I could teach myself with the help of some additional textbooks. The subjects that I knew I was not going to be capable of passing had to be discarded if only to remove the pressure I imposed on myself. My final school report highlighted that I had been absent one hundred and five times during the most crucial time of my education, so this had to be the right decision.

I quickly adapted to the routine of treatment in the radiology clinic. Although each session lasted only a matter of seconds, the physical preparation was precise to a millimetre. Firstly I would lie down with a protective shield placed above me with big blocks made to the exact size of my lungs to protect them from getting any unnecessary damage from the radiation. The shields were placed to line up with every single little tattoo pre- marked on my body. Only when accurately placed could the dose of high energy X-rays begin. For those few seconds I just lay there listening to the sounds of the machines and my instructions to lie still. Like chemotherapy, the radiotherapy was used to destroy all of my blood cells, including the healthy ones, and I became quite anaemic. My doctors wanted me to have a blood transfusion but I was scared of this as it was the late 80's and there was daily media coverage of Aids. I didn't trust that the blood would be screened properly and refused transfusions, opting for a can of Guinness instead. But I'm not that hard really and always had to top it up with a bit of Coke to take away the bitterness. It actually just tasted of shandy and it did work as it brought my red blood count back up and luckily removed the need to receive a transfusion.

Before I went ahead with the radiotherapy, my parents were advised of the risks associated with the location of the treatment. At the time though, we needed to concentrate on treating and curing my existing cancer. But I don't think that they were ever pre-warned of the deadly consequences that the first treatment to cure one cancer would have later in my life by making me especially susceptible to a strike back by cancer in a different form.

7

From ward to award – my final school exams

With the radiotherapy complete I went home and faced my next challenge, my GCSE exams. It was late May and the weather was really heating up. My concentration span was quite limited as I suffered from severe fatigue and needed to get plenty of rest. I only had two days to prepare for my first exam. I knew in my heart that I had done all that I could, given the circumstances, as I sat in the school hall surrounded by my friends and fellow pupils, all sitting in long lines behind one another. I tried to block out my previous six weeks and hoped that the person sitting behind me did not notice the huge bald patch at the back of my head, caused by the radiation that treated the lymph nodes close to my ears. The hall was really warm and I had really excruciating burning sensations underneath my arms, which really distracted me from my exam questions. I sat with my elbows pointing outwards to prevent friction from the rest of my skin. Unfortunately the skin under my arms had been burnt by the radiation and were red raw and very weepy, a very typical side effect, especially in that era because of the dose and field size were both higher than they are now. That caused an immense distraction as I failed to understand the questions on my exam paper. I burst into tears and left the exam hall. I needed to pass these exams to get me on my way to college. Failing simply wasn't an option for me. I managed to compose myself and freshen up before I returned to the hall a few minutes later to make my final attempt at completing the paper.

I did succeed in taking all of my exams, albeit with a few panics along the way. I suffered a huge dose of shingles right at the end of them. My treatment had been so tough and had completely run down my immune system, leaving me quite vulnerable. That dose of shingles made me feel really poorly and my weepy underarms were now accompanied by a semi circular area of little blisters all around my tummy which were equally as painful.

I achieved the grades that I needed to secure my place at college. This determination is certainly a trait that seems to accompany me through life.

8

Career, marriage and miracles

After working hard at college I secured a career in travel and decided to specialise in business travel. I thoroughly enjoyed it. I thrived on the challenges that often confronted me. Each and every working day was never the same. Most of all I felt healthy.

I met Giles on a blind date set up by mutual friends who were actually getting married a couple of weeks later. The four of us met in a pub just outside Tring, in Hertfordshire, and he made me laugh straight away. I remember wearing a pair of navy cotton trousers and a cream paisley top with the most hideous gold chain belt I thought looked really great and trendy at the time. Giles, too, was his normal laid back self, pair of jeans and checked shirt and a huge smile with lovely teeth, which I couldn't help but notice, cemented between his round full cheeks. Not because he was fat - he's actually quite fit and played a lot of football at the time amongst other sporting activities, just kindly dealt a round shaped face just like mine. He was very quick witted and funny, laughed at his own jokes, bit annoying, and although I thought he was very pleasant, I didn't read too much into our relationship going any further. Not until the following Sunday anyway. A gloriously hot sunny day took us to another country pub tucked into the rolling hills in the Hertfordshire countryside, joined with our same friends; you could say it was fate. In the sunshine his blue eyes just sparkled and twinkled and well the rest is history. We married three years later and by our first wedding anniversary we were blessed with our first daughter Olivia, quashing all doubt that I may be infertile due to the chemotherapy. How that moment changed my life and fully enriched it. Like all new mothers I immediately felt this enormous love towards her, wanting to cuddle and stare at her all day long. Olivia looked the spitting image of Giles. She screamed the very moment she was born, her tongue vibrated just like a lizard, perhaps the relief of finally being born by emergency caesarean. Olivia was beautiful and I just wanted to look after her forever.

Twenty months later we were thrilled to have our second daughter, Annabel, born by elective caesarean two weeks early. She was like a porcelain doll, her skin beautiful, soft and peachy and, unlike her sister's arrival, she never murmured, not even to be fed.

I often thought when I was pregnant, what it would be like to love another child just as I loved Olivia, but it all comes so naturally and I love them equally. We hadn't planned to have children so early, in our married life but they are a welcome gift whom we both love dearly. I was always so proud to take them with me to see my consultant at the John Radcliffe on my annual check up appointments when they were young - he was really delighted that I was able to have children and had not encountered any difficulties conceiving.

I was really content with life and mapping out our plans for the future, almost like an itinerary at work, believing what is planned must happen. How misplaced can such presumptions be?

9

Recall

I was thirty three years old – seventeen years after my last treatment – when the Department of Health issued an alert. The ministry asked for all women to come forward who had received mantle radiotherapy during their late teenage years and early twenties. It appeared that there was a link to breast cancer resulting from the radiotherapy to the chest area. It was more prominent in the younger age bracket due to the breast tissue still developing at the time the radiotherapy was administered, thus resulting in tissue damage.

I was recalled to the Churchill Hospital in Oxford for a lengthy consultation with a specialist in which all the risks were discussed with me with regards to breast cancer, lung cancer and damage to the heart. I was shown how to examine myself and what changes to look for. I was also warned of the dangers of smoking as just one cigarette would be equivalent to me smoking a packet due to the damage. This has made me increasingly susceptible to cigarette smoke and I struggle to breathe when someone decides to light one beside me. During the consultation it was concluded that the way forward would be to take advantage of a breast screening programme that the government were going to be launching for all Hodgkin's disease patients, as we were now identified as a special risk group following studies globally. I needed to go back to my doctor and he would arrange for me to be put on a screening programme to have annual mammograms at the local breast screening centre.

For two years I went along for my mammograms and all the results came back clear. I was now in a system where I felt assured that I would be closely monitored and any abnormalities identified immediately.

10

'Good lumps and bad lumps' equals mumbo and jumbo

I'm not a hypochondriac – honest! But during that time of screening I began to feel unwell. Nothing specific, but just not quite right, just as in my teens. I experienced symptoms that are not recognised pointers to breast cancer but which disappeared once I had undergone the first stage of surgery. To add to the perplexities since I didn't have any of the classic symptoms of breast cancer at all; no puckering, dimpling and crusting around the nipples, although the veins in my chest were so clearly visible and looked like a confusing road map. I had a really nasty cough that just went on for months and ended up being diagnosed as asthma. I suffered a cold virtually every week, general aches all over my body, the most horrendous migraines; I had at least two a week. Then there were countless nights when I just had to go to bed because I really felt as though I was going down with flu and then wake up as right as rain in the morning, my body would feel like a furnace, my skin was boiling hot but I was completely frozen inside. I had countless visits to my doctor who started looking at lupus, even rheumatoid arthritis. In the end I actually stopped going to my doctor as I felt like I was really wasting their time. As in the past I knew something wasn't quite right in my body; I felt tired and coughed at the slightest exertion. I had started to examine my body. I had recollections of the feelings that I had had when I had Hodgkin's disease, so I started to feel all my glands – in my neck, under my arms, in my groin. I even tried to feel for lumps in my stomach.

One morning as I got out of bed I had a sharp shooting pain in my chest which made me cry out. It felt as though my whole chest was being crushed for a matter of seconds. But it subsided; I didn't think any more of it, as the day's routines added their distractions.

A couple of days later, after spending the entire day gardening, I prepared for a lovely relaxing bubble bath. When I took my bra off I noticed a pattern on my chest that I had not been aware of before. I thought at the time that it may just be the pattern from my bra. Then, in the bath, as I was washing myself, I felt a really tiny lump in my left breast. I don't think it felt any bigger than the size of a pea. I moved around a little and tried to find the lump again and actually struggled to. Then I felt it again. I was on my own that evening. Giles had gone to watch England play the first football match at the new Wembley Stadium. As I got into bed that evening I felt the lump again, so I knew that it was definitely there. Although I was concerned, I wasn't excessively alarmed. In the back of my mind I had the knowledge that I was on a screening programme. Therefore, all abnormalities and changes would be recognised at the outset, preventing anything to develop. In bed I had to raise my arm above my head to feel the lump with ease, and it only took a very gently touch to feel. It was a Friday evening and as I lay in bed waiting for Giles to come home my mind became preoccupied with wanting him to feel what I was feeling. And no doubt about it he could.

It was the beginning of June. I was due to have my next mammogram the following month. There was no way that I was going to allow myself to wait that long. On the Monday morning I managed to get an appointment with a locum in my doctor's surgery. In many ways I didn't actually believe that anything would be wrong, and when I was examined by the doctor he almost mirrored my thoughts. "It feels like a good lump and you get to know what a good lump and a bad lump feels like," he said. "… but because of your medical history we will refer you to a breast care specialist." "Great," I thought, and walked out completely assured. I had nothing to worry about. It was after all a good lump!

I went home and continued with the routine of my life; oblivious to the sinister companion I had inside me. In a few days I received a letter for my appointment for a mammogram and to see a breast consultant at my local hospital. My appointment was for the end of the following week, within the guidelines of the service pledge that everyone must be seen by a specialist within two weeks of presenting a lump with their doctor. In the days leading to my appointment it was really strange: there seemed to be so much coverage on TV about breast cancer. It was on daytime TV; in the news in particular there was a story about a lady trying to get her local health authority to allow her to receive Herceptin to treat her type of cancer. There were even posters up in our local shop saying it was good to talk about cancer. There were posters promoting the Race for Life as well. I seemed to be surrounded with it. It was numbing and surreal.

The following Friday morning, believing that there would be nothing wrong, I made the decision to go to hospital on my own and told Giles I would be absolutely fine. "Just go to work, it's really not worth you taking time off to come with me," I told him.

11

The broom cupboard

As I drove that morning to Bedford Hospital, my local hospital in the South East of England, I was alone. I didn't need Giles by my side as I hoped that my visit would be a short one and confirm my doctor's initial opinion. "It was going to be a good lump." The sun was shining but there was a chill in the air; it was still early. I remember wearing a long white linen skirt and a lemon top with a matching cardigan. My mum's always told me to put something smart on when you are seeing a 'consultant', almost like putting on your Sunday best.

I found with ease the waiting room for the mammo-gram and was surprised that it was such a small room, almost like a little broom cupboard, furnished with half a dozen chairs and a small table with a limited selection of magazines. I must have been the first patient that morning as I was called very promptly by the radiographer, an older lady with blonde hair worn in a bun. She smiled and spoke to me constantly as I undressed to the waist.

"You look bright and summery today - it's a beautiful day out there isn't it?" she said, before she quizzed me on the position of the lump, in preparation for the mammogram, an x ray picture of my breast. "You'll be going next door for an ultra sound when you have finished in here," she informed me.

"Is that normal?" I asked. "I don't usually have an ultra sound during my annual screening."

"We like to give everyone an ultra sound when they come in for their mammogram," she replied. Having the mammogram was slightly uncomfortable but certainly wasn't painful and actually over with relatively quickly. Then, as I got dressed to go and sit in the waiting area for the ultra sound, I thanked her. I thought perhaps the reason for the ultra sound was due to me presenting a lump - it was just an additional precautionary measure.

As I lay on the couch, stripped to the waist again, the cold gel smothered across my chest, I watched the screen beside me as another radiographer, a man of few words, glided the transducer across my chest. He appeared to be measuring what looked like chewing gum on the screen as he scanned me. Thankfully my initial radiographer was in the room with me holding my hand. There were a couple of shadowy areas that he focused on and was very thorough as he took his time. I lay there silently, unsure of any questions to ask. The ultrasound was building up a picture of my breast and would be able to identify if the lump was solid and made up of cells, or if it was likely to be a cyst which would be filled with fluid. Once the ultra sound was complete, the gel wiped off, I dressed. "Just take a seat outside while we print the images and report for you to take to the consultant," the radiographer said, smiling at me. As instructed I sat outside, the corridor empty and silent, and waited for the images and report to be printed.

When the radiographer opened the door and handed my files to me, she squeezed my hand. "Take care of yourself sweetheart." I suppose at that moment it should have triggered alarm bells. It didn't. I felt she was being kind to me. After all, mine was a good lump, so I just continued naively along the long narrow corridor and up the stairs to the out-patient department where I saw a member of the breast care team.

12

The bombshell

I reported to reception and handed over my files.

"Take a seat, clinic is running late today but we will see you as quickly as we can," the receptionist advised. I turned around to a busy waiting room, every seat occupied with women of all sorts of shape, size and age. Some on their own, like me, but others had friends with them for moral support, engaged in deep conversation. The clinic was running an hour late. I tried to engross myself with all the magazines on offer, while glancing at other patients as they were called in to see the consultants and then strolled out what felt like moments later.

Then my name was called. Unsure of what to expect, I entered the consulting room to be met by a middle aged, quietly spoken registrar and a nurse as his assistant. I thought I would be asked to take another seat. I don't recall an introduction, only being told, "…pop into the examination room and get undressed to the waist. I am going to do a needle aspiration test and a core biopsy. Please don't worry because I will give you a local anaesthetic so you won't feel anything."

I wasn't expecting that. The needle test would involve the withdrawal of cells from the lump through a fine needle and into a syringe to be sent to the lab for testing for cancer cells. A hollow needle is used to remove and almost shred a sample of tissue during the biopsy and that tissue could be looked at under a microscope to see if it is normal or abnormal. Not properly registering in detail, I asked practically, "…will I be able to drive home afterwards because I have come to hospital on my own?"

The response: "What, you have come to hospital on your own? No you won't be able to drive home."

The good lump suddenly seemed less bouncy.

I lay on the couch and, as the registrar performed the test, I asked, "So do you think it is a cyst then?"

"No it's not a cyst" was the reply. I now know the radiographers write their own report from the mammogram and ultra sound with a grading of the likelihood of cancer. So I suppose he knew what he was dealing with in advance. What alarmed me at that point was the sternness in which he asked the nurse to contact the lab to see how quickly it would be able to get the results back from my test. Unfortunately, the lab staff was not available.

"Page them then," he asserted. "You can't keep a patient waiting."

Realising how seriously something seemed to be amiss, I started shaking. My teeth were chattering, just as they had when I lay petrified of having my caesareans. Feeling numb, I dressed.

"Please go and get yourself a coffee and then come back and we will have the results for you," he instructed me.

"How long are they likely to be?" I asked.

"About an hour," he replied.

As soon as I walked out of the room I unconsciously ignored all of the 'do not use mobile phone' signs and dialled Giles immediately. I needed him to be with me. Something wasn't right. He answered but before he had the opportunity to say anything further, I said "please can you come to hospital? I've had some tests and I can't drive home. Something is wrong. I need you with me."

He could tell by the tone in my voice that I was on the verge of panic. He assured me that he would be with me as quickly as he could.

I went downstairs for a coffee in the Bistro Cafe where I sat for what seemed an eternity, watching the hospital staff, visitors and patients taking lunch. I sat alone with my vacant thoughts, feeling chilled to the bone.

As soon as I finished my coffee I made my way back to the out-patients' department. It was deserted at lunch time. So I sat there on my own waiting in a daze. I couldn't even pick up a magazine to read. I felt quite cold in my summery clothes, probably coupled with an element of shock over the tests. I gradually became aware it must have been two o'clock as the afternoon clinic patients started to arrive for their appointments, and they were being directed where to sit and wait.

I overheard a nurse shout that the results weren't back yet and automatically assumed that they were referring to me. Giles had still not arrived. Then a nurse called "Sarah-Jane Phillips." I got up and returned to the same consultancy room. As I walked in, the registrar looked at me, stood up and walked towards me, took my hand and said "it's not good news, I'm afraid."

I looked at him and replied, "I know. I overheard someone say that the results weren't back yet."

He replied, "No we have your results and it's cancer."

The numbness returned. Suddenly I wasn't in front of him anymore. Instead my mind just clouded over and froze. I wanted comfort and escaped to flashes of Olivia and Annabel before me. They would be expecting me to collect them from school shortly and take them to the certain familiarity of home. One moment I was in a daze, the next my head spun with terrible prospects. How they would cope without me? I didn't want them to be wandering around in the playground, waiting for me. Lianne, my neighbour and one of my truest friends, was the first person I thought of for help. I'd call her, ask her to collect them, take them home, give them a biscuit and a drink, and look after them until I got home. They were only five and seven at the time. How could I be taken from them so young? In moments of shock, practicalities elbow into your mind; they thankfully never fail you.

Then I sat down and the registrar held my hand as he discussed my results. The clinic nurse made me a cup of tea with sugar in it, terribly British I know, almost as if it was going to eliminate my worst fears. Both the registrar and nurse showed me lots of compassion and empathy as they tried to reassure me that I had done the right thing examining myself as it was in the early stages, and explained and drew diagrams on how breast cancer develops and spreads. I was not capable of taking in a thing and just looked at them blankly. Tears were streaming down my face. Why did that locum doctor tell me it felt like a good lump? Then Giles arrived and was ushered into the room to me. I got up, looked at him and said, "it's cancer."

He immediately broke into tears.

"I'm sorry for not coming to hospital and being here for you," he said.

"It's ok," I kept telling him, "it's in the early stages."

Not really having a clue what this actually meant really and just picking it out as a positive comment that the registrar had used. The registrar continued drawing diagrams for Giles to understand as well and went on to tell us that I would probably just need to go on and have a lumpectomy. It would involve removing the lump surgically, and then I would go on to have radiotherapy. To be honest, we couldn't really take in too much information as we were both in total shock. I tried to be brave for Giles and thought how I was going to communicate everything to the girls, how I was going to tell my parents. They didn't even know that I had found a lump let alone had a hospital appointment that day.

With the registrar telling me everything he could for the moment, he made me another appointment for the following week to meet the breast surgeon when more of my results would be known. In the meantime, I was sent home with a pile of literature on breast cancer. If I said I did any bedtime reading I would seriously be lying. I never turned a page.

13

Next to you

Imust have floated back to the car, almost detaching myself from reality. I felt absolutely numb with such a huge amount of uncertainty ahead for me. I tried to be brave for Giles, to hide my fear to shelter him so he didn't feel so frightened. I wanted him to be strong for the children.

We decided to stop at my parents' house on the way home as we were passing it. I knew that I needed to share the heartbreaking news with them. "What do I say to them? How do I tell them? How do I choose the right words?" I kept asking Giles. Nothing will ever prepare you so you choose the right language to tell the people you love the most that you have cancer. For my parents it would be a huge reminder after my first encounter; they would probably feel that I had a massive injustice befall me.

As we pulled up onto the drive my dad was doing some work in the garage and looked surprised to see the both of us. Mum was equally surprised, working away in the kitchen, puzzled that we were alone at the time when I should be collecting the children from school.

"Mum, dad I've got something to tell you." I had to be direct."I found a lump and I have been to hospital this morning for some tests and they have confirmed that I have breast cancer, but it's ok, I'm ok, and I've been told that it is in the early stages."

I still did not cry. My dad continued to stand before me, stunned and silent, but my mum collapsed momentarily at the shock. Everyone reacts differently to shock. Giles and I looked at each other as he then proceeded to make us all a cup of tea with sugar. I think we all needed it. Mum managed to get back on her feet and she had within seconds demonstrated how she needed me to be strong. I didn't really have anything else of substance to tell them because I didn't actually know any more myself.

We didn't really stay there for very long. I had to leave mum and dad and allow them time to reflect and digest the events of the day. I was really keen to get home to my girls. When Giles had gone out of the kitchen to the car my dad took me by the hand and said one thing to me, "You've got to be strong because Giles needs you to be strong and the girls need you to be strong, too." Then he gave me a hug and I got into the car and we drove home - the place where I had always felt safe and protected from the threats of the outside world.

The first thing we did when we arrived home was open a bottle of red wine and we both sat there and cried uncontrollably in each other's arms, pouring ourselves another glass as it slipped down really easily.

"What if it's terminal?" I kept asking him. "I'm not ready to die yet."

Giles has always been the optimist, always positive and has been from this moment. He just couldn't comprehend those words. I felt emotionally exhausted; the day had taken its toll on me.

The girls were at Lianne's having dinner which she kindly volunteered doing but I needed to go and get them, desperate to spend every moment with them. Suddenly, I became really strong as I wiped away my tears and regained my composure to collect them. They were far too young to understand and I couldn't allow them to worry about me. I gave Lianne a kiss. "Thank you for having them and giving them dinner, I'll speak to you later." Then I picked up their school bags and lunch boxes, and took them both home. I suggested that the three of us have a bath together as soon as we got in and we just sat in it, chatting and laughing. On occasion they quizzed me over the small dressing covering the biopsy area. "What's that mummy, why is it there?" they asked. "Oh I just scratched myself; it's nothing to worry about," I told them, desperately trying to carry on as normal, for their sake, and succeeding.

With the girls tucked up in bed it was important for me to make a couple of phone calls to my closest friends to let them know of the outcome of my day. I knew those phone calls would be difficult and tearful. Initially they were shocked, slightly unsure of what to say but within moments they focused on the positives and did their best to reassure me. Their positive words filled me with so much hope.

That night I didn't get a moment of sleep, I just lay next to Giles as closely as I could and cried the entire night. My life literally flashed before me as I felt that my days were numbered. Furthermore I had just finished reading "Next to You" by Gloria Hunniford, about her daughter Caron Keating's lost battle with breast cancer. I feared that was going to happen to me. I had cried so much reading it; I couldn't possibly imagine how terrible and catastrophic it must be to leave such young children behind.

14

Déjà vu

The following day, we were due to go to the christening of my friend's daughter in West Malling, Kent. I have been friends with Kathryn for many years now and I was excited that she had chosen to return from New York to have her daughter Hannah christened. In actual fact it was Kathryn and her mum and dad who were the first people that I had told of my Hodgkin's disease and there we were exactly twenty years to the month later and I was telling them of the breast cancer. It was as if time had stood still. We'd covered this path before, and yet I had done and achieved so much in that time.

During the morning I had reservations about facing people, irrespective of being friends or not, as I didn't think that I could find the resources to stay strong in front of them. Particularly as these celebratory gatherings are filled with acquaintances of days gone by where pleasantries are almost ritualistic: "Hi how are you? You look really well... haven't seen you for ages... what are you up to now?"

I could really do without the small talk, especially today when everything was all so raw and honest; answers would be brutal on an otherwise joyous occasion. I wanted to curl myself up into a tight ball and feel sorry for myself. The prospect of dressing up felt all too much for me.

My parents really encouraged me to go along, feeling that it would be beneficial for me to go and be with people I was fond of, to help take my mind of things for a few hours. The alternative would be to sit at home and worry about all the terrible unknowns.

We did make the christening and standing in church that afternoon, surrounded by some familiar faces, I closed my eyes and prayed just for a few moments that I would be ok, as the tears started to fill my eyes. I wanted to be here to help and watch my little girls grow into beautiful young ladies and it was my responsibility and purpose in life to ensure that I fulfil that role. At that moment I never wanted anyone else to stand in my shoes. The reception afterwards was held at home and I tried really hard to mingle and socialise with old friends but my mind was distracted and preoccupied with concerns that I had no control over as I stood amongst the joviality from all the other guests. I just felt bereft, my stomach in knots and my body tingled from head to toe. I was still in complete shock.

15

Awaiting sentence

The week that followed my diagnosis, undoubtedly the longest week of my life, was almost like waiting for sentence to be passed, as I waited for my appointment with the breast consultant, I lost the ability to function, my body in complete shock. Amazingly, I managed to get the girls up and dressed for school, made their packed lunches and served them breakfast, walked them to school: they chattered away to each other, oblivious of the situation. But as soon as I left them in the playground I turned my back and my world crumbled, unable to stop the tears from falling as I walked home. Thankfully I wasn't on my own for long. My mum and dad came round every day with all the ironing and a tray of food with an evening meal for everyone. I didn't have an appetite and couldn't stomach any food so the prospect of serving up a family meal was a massive incapability for me. I survived on cups of tea with half a sugar! Just what the paramedic ordered!

My parents spent every day with me. They pottered around the house and tried getting me doing chores to take my mind off things. But as soon as the end of the school day arrived I needed to compose myself and collect the girls, send mum and dad home and act out a sense of normality, for their sake.

It was the Friday morning when we returned to the hospital to meet my breast consultant, a pleasant but frank man with quite a dry disposition. This man would ultimately be the one responsible for saving my life, the man who would cut me open and remove the cancerous growth that currently invaded my body. Within minutes of meeting him, I knew I could trust his self-confident and authoritative manner. Immediately I sensed that he was well respected, but he was just about to deal me my first blow. He started reiterating everything that the registrar had discussed with me the previous week, highlighting my quick action to respond when I found the suspicious lump, before swiftly moving on to the basic facts.

"As you have had mantle radiotherapy to treat Hodgkin's disease in your chest this means that you have had the maximum amount of radiotherapy to that area that you can receive in your lifetime. Now radiotherapy is one of the treatments that we use to treat breast cancer and as we can't give you this treatment your cancer will have a forty percent chance of recurrence."

I didn't even look at Giles; my gut instinct just knew what was coming next. I immediately said, "just get rid of it then, I'll have a mastectomy." I had to be decisive.

He looked at me and replied. "That is what I am thinking and it will be the best thing for you to do."

Giles, on the other hand, was completely shocked; he wasn't expecting that news and kept focus – on the positive. "But it's got a sixty percent chance of not coming back."

"Not interested Giles – forty percent risk is much too high a risk. I'm only thirty six," I blurted. "I can't worry about this for the rest of my life."

One moment we were talking about a mastectomy, completely losing my breast, and the next moment the conversation moved really quickly on to breast reconstruction.

"We will be able to perform the reconstruction at the same time as the mastectomy," said my consultant.

Unsure, I asked, "What do most people do?"

My consultant looked at me, really vaguely, almost with disbelief in his eyes, and replied: "It doesn't matter what most people do. It matters what you want to do. I am more than happy to refer you to a plastic surgeon who will carry out this procedure."

As he was offering the reconstruction, I thought that it would be a good idea to go along and at least have a consultation; after all I didn't really understand what the reconstruction was or what it would entail. My level of comprehension was incredibly limited, but I did understand that it would be this man, my breast surgeon, who would remove my breast and then a plastic surgeon would take over and make me a new one to replace it.

"If you are going to go ahead with this I will make you an appointment with the plastic surgeon for next week so you can decide what you would like to do," the breast surgeon said. I agreed.

In that consultation also present was the breast care nurse, a really petite lady with very short fair hair, who smiled kindly at me at intervals during my appointment. She spoke to me afterwards in her soft tone with empathy and reassurance, deeply trying to understand exactly how I felt.

"How have you got on this week? How have you been feeling?" she enquired

"I'm in a daze - still in shock. I can't really explain how I feel," I told her. "My mind is constantly preoccupied; I don't know what is going to happen to me."

"It's difficult for you in the beginning but you will start to feel more positive. I will call you in the next few days to arrange for you to come and see me in the Primrose Unit and I will also make an appointment for you to see the oncologist. I'll do my best to get the appointments close together."

The Primrose Unit at Bedford Hospital is the oncology department. It is where all of the chemotherapy is administered.

It was that day that the complexity of breast cancer struck home, particularly as I was now going ahead with a mastectomy - a much more radical surgical procedure than originally expected. Giles and I left that appointment with the harsh reality of what exactly breast cancer entailed and the huge impact that it would play on our life from that moment on.

Giles didn't go to work for the rest of the day. Instead, we went and had a couple of glasses of therapeutic red wine in our local pub and just tried to come to terms with the daunting implications of the morning's news – how the road ahead was filled with so much uncertainty. I don't like red wine that much but there are times when you need to succumb to the cloudy mood it has over you.

"I can't believe this is happening I can't imagine what it will be like for you," Giles said as he held my hand and gave me a gentle kiss on the cheek, as we sat oblivious to everything around us.

I was adamant that I wanted to retain complete normality as far as the girls were concerned; they didn't need to know what mummy had. To them I would function as normal and as they were accustomed too. So the next day, I took myself off to Sainsbury's and left them with Giles so I could do the shopping without them traipsing around with me. I was in that shop for three hours walking aimlessly up and down the aisles in a complete trance not having a clue what to buy. What I do recall though is spending two hundred and thirty four pounds and not having a single thing to put a meal together when I unpacked the shopping bags when I returned home!

I was alright; I still couldn't stomach any food, opting to drink sugared tea. I started to lose a little bit of weight and friends in the playground told me how well I was looking. "Well done you," they said. All I could do was look at them and say "thank you." I didn't want to engage in small talk, no matter how well intended.

16

How do I tell my children?

A few weeks previously I had been happy playing out the continuing narrative we call life and its full expectancies. Now my life was turned upside down as I was catapulted into the hospital system, my diary commitments replaced with seeing the breast care nurse one day, the oncologist the next and the plastic surgeon the following day.

I met the breast care nurse in the Primrose Unit with Giles. Oddly, I didn't notice anything about the unit or the patients. I just looked straight ahead of me as we reported in at reception and was told to take the lift to the first floor. I didn't want to look around as I was scared of facing anyone looking seriously ill. When the lift doors opened on the first floor and the breast care nurse met us it was like walking onto a corridor of offices, a reminder of the world I was familiar with, and she took us through to a small room with a table and four comfy chairs around it and offered us a cup of tea. Now I wasn't going to pass on tea with sugar! I couldn't help but notice all of the leaflets, DVD's on display, information helping people cope with their cancer diagnosis, but I refused to take any home with me. I was blocking it out, not accepting that it was happening to me.

In the short term Giles was really worried about me not eating as I was feeling nauseous the whole time. I told the nurse.

"It's perfectly natural to feel like that but when you are ready just eat something that you really fancy, even if it is a little piece of chocolate or a biscuit," she advised. Now I know where my love of smooth Galaxy chocolate comes from after being given the virtual green light to go for it. It was during this meeting, after going through some general formalities, the kindness, the gentle touches of compassion, the empathy, reassurance that you are in good hands; the nurse indicated the worst to me.

"They are really going to throw chemotherapy at you. I'm sure that they will give you as much as they can because you are young and your body will be able to cope with it."

"Do you think I will need to have chemotherapy then?" I asked, immediately thinking of Giles and the girls, and looking ugly if I lost my hair. I probably asked what every woman asks at that point. "Am I going to lose my hair? Will it all fall out?"

"The type of chemotherapy that you will have will definitely make your hair fall out. But you can get some beautiful wigs these days and there are lots of scarves available to look at downstairs before you go." She was doing her best to reassure me that I would look fine.

"Ok, so losing your hair is one thing but what about my eyelashes, will my eyelashes fall out because they can't as I always need to wear mascara?" My question gave way to a panicked tone. I don't know what the nurse must have thought of me, newly diagnosed with breast cancer but really worrying about being able to wear mascara or not.

"Some people lose them, some people just don't" was the answer she gave me.

"What do I tell my girls?" I asked her. How much do they need to know? They are only little and they won't understand. I don't want to frighten them."

Clearly, I needed to tell them something as they would be able to see the physical changes that would be taking place with me and I need to tell them at their level of understanding without causing alarm.

"I can put you in touch with someone who was diagnosed with breast cancer at around your age and also had young children, if you would like?" she asked.

"That would be a nice, thank you." Refreshing, sorry I know not quite the word to have in mind, to know that someone else had gone through it in the same situation as me.

"Please please", I started to say, "I am happy to take all of the treatment that you throw my way. But, if there is ever any bad news to hear or anything unpleasant to be told, I don't want to know about, I'm really not strong enough to deal with this emotionally. So if you have anything to tell me please contact Giles first," I told her, then looked at Giles. "Is that ok with you?"

He nodded, terrified himself!

From a young age, I have always had a fear of dying. It is something that I am petrified about because of the sadness that it leaves behind. I don't want my children to feel that sense of loss. I still have this fear to this day. The nurse did sympathise with me and understood what I said and I really believe that that comment was passed onto all concerned, eventually.

17

First impressions can be misleading

The following day I took my mum with me for my first appointment with the oncologist. Thank heavens I did. If I had been on my own I really don't know what I would have done to him. We were back in the Primrose Unit and for the first time we needed to have a seat in the waiting area: quite a bright room with full view of everyone walking in and out of the unit, the majority being much older than myself. I was exceptionally anxious about my appointment and didn't engage with anyone in the room and didn't make any further observations. I had dealt with oncologists in the past and just sitting waiting brought back all the memories of how sick I had been having chemo. We were called through by a nurse and shown into a consulting room where a door was opened and closed behind us as we entered.

"The oncologist will be with you shortly." This nurse quietly spoke. Sitting in that consulting room with my mum I just felt cold and started shaking. We must have waited for what felt like fifteen minutes before a distracted oncologist walked through another door without an apology for keeping us waiting. I was completely put off by this and took an instant dislike to him. I know that these people are extremely clever and the highest credit given for dedicating their lives to the field of research. Let's face it, he was clearly very good at conversing with cells, but he had absolutely no skill of dealing with people with very fragile emotions. His distance, the absence of any kind of bedside manner, his poor communication skills at first meeting him, frightened me. I would never be able to build any kind of rapport. He was unprepared for me. He didn't have my medical records, which actually wasn't his fault, and to me he appeared to be noticeably thinking on his feet, without apparent appreciation for the consequences of what he was saying.

I quote one remark that is engrained in my memory. "Well you can't have radiotherapy - this is a treatment we use for breast cancer. The chemotherapy that you had previously may have damaged your heart." I knew this from the breast surgeon so why was he repeating a negative? He added abruptly. "Do you know what kind of chemotherapy you had last time?" *I'd been a child, for goodness sake.*

I shook my head.

"It may mean that we won't be able to use the chemo-therapy that we use to treat breast cancer either."

I burst into tears, believing that there was nothing that they could do for me. This is it - I'm going to die. They can't treat me.

"Look," I said, "you just have to be able to treat me. I have two little girls at home. They need me to be here for them. You must be able to treat me."

Then he piped up "It's ok; it will be ok. We can use other combinations of drugs to treat you. There are lots of options available to us. You will be fine – we'll be able to come up with something for you."

Why didn't he just say that to begin with? I could not believe that he could be so insensitive to a patient without having any knowledge of their medical history and personality.

He was continuing, "…I do think it would be a good idea if you have an echocardiogram to ensure that your heart is ok and fit for chemotherapy, though. I'll send you an appointment in the post."

"So I will definitely be having chemotherapy then?" I needed confirmation, though I would have been happy to escape the side effects

"Yes - it is invasive cancer and you will need to have between four and six sessions, depending on the results after your surgery."

As we got up to leave, I tried to offer some organisation towards what lay ahead. "I will phone up my old professor and ensure that they send my medical files to you as soon as possible, so you can decide what chemotherapy will be best for me."

He just smiled at me and shook my hand. "I'll see you again after your surgery."

As I left the consulting room, with my mum, I felt physically exhausted and mentally drained. That wasn't what I had expected of a first meeting. I wanted to feel safe and looked after and I didn't sense that. Instead, he had petrified me. The chemo nurses obviously knew his manner and were attentive; they smiled at me and reassured me that everything would be fine. Chemotherapy acted like my insurance policy. In other words it was precautionary and if there were any stray cells invisible to the naked eye after surgery it would destroy them.

This was only my first impression of this oncologist.

18

The first of many

The following afternoon I returned to the out-patients' department to see the plastic surgeon who would take me to the vital stage of reconstruction. I was becoming more familiar with the department now. It was pretty soulless and dull, and quite claustrophobic, almost sitting on top of the other patients in the waiting room. Some of them moaned that they had been waiting for so long to be seen by the consultant. I felt anxious and apprehensive as I waited, but I sought comfort having Giles beside me, my extra pair of ears that were alert to something I might miss. We grew accustomed to the clinic times over-running and, although we sat there patiently, that waiting game surfaced all of my emotions. I sat rocking in an attempt to comfort myself until my name was called and we walked into yet another consulting room where we were greeted.

"Hello, Fred Schreuder," the surgeon introduced himself. I always remember that introduction because he never prefixed his name with 'Mr', and he said his first name, an indication that he was going to be approachable.

We sat for a few moments as he explored any previous operations I may have had in the past and quizzed us to confirm that we had completed our family, giving him more options in surgical procedures that would be available to me if I chose to go down the line of reconstruction. Then he examined me to establish my suitability for surgery. He measured the fat on my stomach, an option he could use as a donor site. That might actually be one of the only moments in my life when I have been quite happy with an extra bit of insulation around my tummy. You just never know when you are going to need it. I lost the baby weight with Olivia really easily but had always struggled after Annabel. Perhaps that was just meant to be as I was holding onto it for this eventuality. When I got myself dressed and sat down again beside Giles I just didn't have the brain capacity to take in what was coming next. Mr Schreuder started to describe in great detail all of the types of reconstructions that would be available and which he felt would be the best option for me. He described it as the 'crème de la crème' of reconstructions, 'The Free Tram DIEP flap.' This is one of the most advanced forms of breast reconstruction.

The surgery would involve removing muscle, skin and fat from my stomach with the blood vessels attached and disconnecting the blood supply, before inserting this tissue into the breast socket after all my breast tissue had been removed and reconnecting the blood supply by fusing the blood vessels together using micro surgery.

This would be the most aesthetically pleasing for me and he was going to be more than happy for me to have this procedure. But, it would need to be done at The Lister Hospital in Stevenage, twenty minutes from where I live and also our local centre of excellence for plastic surgery. It is particularly equipped for microsurgery. It was also the most lengthy of procedures being between ten and twelve hours to perform. Tears streamed down my face. How could such a tiny lump be the cause of so much intervention? Not only did this type of procedure terrify me beyond belief, I also have a massive fear of anaesthetics. There was no way that I would be able to put myself through that length of surgery. Was it that important for what is a cosmetic procedure in the end? I'd had enough, incapable of making any kind of rational decision.

Mr Schreuder obviously understood. "I'm not expecting you to make a decision today. Why don't you go home and think about it and come back and see me next week, when you have had time to make up your mind" He added: "Think of any questions you may have." He never lost eye contact.

I have never established if it was the procedure that frightened me or the length of time that I would be under an anaesthetic that terrified me more. Neither do I know if I have built this enormous fear of the anaesthetic because I could not deal with what happened to me once I was put to sleep.

What a week I had. So much daunting medical jargon needed taking in all because of this pea sized foreign invasion in my left boob. I believed that I wasn't strong or brave enough to put myself through such a long complex operation to restore my body to what had always defined me as feminine and a woman. My initial feelings were to have a mastectomy, get rid of the foe within and move on with life. It's not important in the scheme of staring death in the face. I returned home and immediately accessed the internet for pictures of women who have undergone breast surgery without reconstruction. My heart sank into the deepest pit of my stomach. I really didn't want to look anything like that. A personal choice I appreciate, but one I just wasn't quite ready to face at my age. The alternative: the long anaesthetic with all the complications that could entail, with the end result a natural looking, warm soft breast to replace the one I was about to lose and the long term psychological benefit in aiding a full recovery.

Casting the shadow over any decision was still my fear of being put to sleep for so long. What if it went wrong, they couldn't bring me round and I died on the operating table. In my dad's quirkiness, he told me, "hey what a way to go. You won't feel a thing and you will be none the wiser!"

It just ate away at me though. I was so anxious. Giles wiped away the tears and just listened to my huge reluctance for days on end, until he reached the end of his tether. "You know I love you more than anything whatever you decide, but I know you better than anybody else and I know if you don't have the reconstruction you won't be happy with yourself."

He was right; I already knew what I didn't want to look like.

The doorbell didn't stop ringing as my friends came with bars of Galaxy chocolate to offer their support and advice, trying so desperately hard to understand how I felt and what I was going through. I hated playing the vulnerable victim in front of them as I cried in their arms. We had such deep meaningful conversations that felt so premature in our time of life that have deepened our friendships and touched us today. The general consensus was if they were in my position they would unquestionably opt for the reconstruction. Then, in a quiet conversation with my dad, he mentioned "it wouldn't make any difference if you are under for two hours or ten hours, you won't know anything about it and you can get it all over with in one operation and this time next year it will all be over and you will be able to put everything behind you."

I knew this all made sense in many ways I just had to break down the barrier of fear.

With my mind made up I drove myself back to hospital to see Mr Schreuder. I didn't have an appointment time. Instead, I had been told to get to the clinic at two o'clock and I would be slotted in at a time when the consultant was free. The clinic ended up being extremely busy. Everyone complained to one another. One was a local councillor and, full of self-importance, thought it would be advantageous for him to put his councillor badge around his neck, hoping that would help him to be seen more quickly. He complained it was outrageous that he had to wait and he was going to take it up with the *Bedfordshire On Sunday*, our free weekly local newspaper. He blamed his inconvenience on the breast cancer patients, who he claimed took priority. He had a dodgy finger and I had to bite my tongue to refrain from telling him to swivel on it. I had to sit there for about an hour and a half and listen to his drivel. I ended up being the very last person in clinic, having waited three hours when I was called in to see Mr Schreuder.

As soon as I walked into the consulting room, the same room I visited the previous week, I could feel the tears welling up inside me stirring my deep emotions, as I so bravely told him that I would go ahead with the procedure that he recommended would be the best option for me.

"Sarah, I'm confident in performing this operation and it carries a ninety five percent success rate. It will be the most anaesthetically pleasing and nobody will be able to tell the difference. It will be absolutely perfect. But I won't be able to operate for about six weeks."

He went through his diary and gave me an approximate date. His confidence contributed towards assuaging my fears though, but as I left the appointment I cried. The trolley wheels were to be put in motion; I always stand by my decisions and from that moment on there would be no going back on my part.

So in four weeks my life had been turned upside down. At innumerable out-patient appointments, I was bombarded with so much information, unable to take everything in. My technique for coping was to discard what I knew I couldn't deal with and my mind switched off.

Mr Schreuder telephoned after the consultation to confirm the operation date. Typically, the day we were due to go on holiday, just another confirmation of the cruel intrusion by rampant cells.

Waiting for the surgery date to arrive imposed another level of stress on me. I felt so scared of having the lump inside me growing every second it was left. I needed to call the breast care nurse to seek some reassurance at the delay. She knew me instantly on the phone and was very calm with me. She understood my concerns but reassured me that everything was absolutely fine, they knew what they were dealing with, it was in the early stages and quite small and it's not going to grow too much in the time frame given.

My pre-operative assessment shortly followed at the Lister Hospital where I met the sister in charge of the plastics ward for the first time. She gave me a tour of the hospital ward and explained that I would be in a room on my own due to the nature of the surgery and I would be close to the nurses' station if there were any problems. She also reinforced my understanding of the type of surgery that I was having and what would happen to me after surgery, and explained that I would have drains in my stomach and chest to take away the oedema. So that I fully understood what would happen to me she also had some books and leaflets at her disposal for Giles and myself to have a look at. They were examples of other reconstructions to try and help me understand what I was going to look like afterwards. Giles and I looked at each other and he held my hand, and I just needed to speak out. "That's not the operation that I'm having because that's not perfect and I've been told that mine will be absolutely perfect!"

The scar lines on the pictures just looked really puckered to me like badly kneaded pastry dough, and I didn't want to look like that.

"What on earth are we doing?" I was shocked and ill prepared.

"You're going to be cut open. Wherever you are cut you are going to have a scar, but over time those scars will fade," the sister replied, trying to soften the blow. We walked out of the hospital, confused and trance-like.

19

Hannah Montana

With a couple of weeks free from hospital appointments before my date for surgery, we decided to escape to Jersey for a week, to stay with family. It did us the world of good to get away. We wouldn't be able to have a holiday for the next few months so it just seemed the ideal time to go. It also gave me the perfect opportunity to spend quality time with the girls - try to explain to them what would happen to mummy in the coming months in a way that they understood. I didn't want to cause any unnecessary worry for them.

If it wasn't for cancer we would have had the perfect week. We were so lucky with the weather, having glorious sunshine every day of our stay. It allowed us to just frolic around on the beach and share some really special times. They were spoilt only by the moments in the back of my mind when I couldn't help but feel that I may be seeing things for the last time. I might not be here next year, a little voice in my head would say. When we left anywhere, I admit, I took a few moments to take everything in, just in case it was going to be for the last time.

With only a couple of days to go before our return I knew I needed to say something to the girls. I couldn't procrastinate any more. I didn't sit down and rehearse anything, instead I thought on my feet and, luckily, I don't think I could have done any better. After having lunch at one of our favourite restaurants, The Old Courthouse in St Aubins, we made our way back to the car and I chose that moment to tell them as I hugged them.

"You know mummy had a little injection in her booby a little while ago?"

"Yes" they said.

"Well, the doctors found something in mummy's booby that shouldn't be there and I will need to have an operation to have it taken out."

They didn't really understand and I could tell that it wasn't really registering with them, "...and after the operation mummy is going to have some really nasty medicine to make me better. But that medicine will make mummy feel a little bit poorly and will also make my hair fall out." My voice softened as I said those last few words.

I paused and watched Olivia gulp. I don't know how I managed to keep control and not cry at that moment but managed to go on to say "...but don't worry because mummy is going to have a long blonde wig just like Hannah Montana!"

I had no idea where that came from. They could relate to Hannah Montana wearing a wig and that explanation appeared to ease the shock of it all. For those of you that do not know, Hannah Montana is a Disney character who is Miley Cyrus by day, a normal teenager, and by night she turns into a singing megastar and puts on a long blonde wig! The girls were really taken by her at the time and my association with her had worked a trick. Although I can't see myself ever bursting into song! They didn't ask me any more questions and outwardly appeared to understand everything I said.

On our last evening, we sat around the table for dinner. There were fifteen of us, all Giles' family, and various conversations were taking place naturally when so many people get together. There are moments in life that you never forget. That evening was one of them. It was the first time that I have seen Giles sob so emotionally it scared me – I knew he was scared, too – of potentially losing me. As Giles looked at me across the table he couldn't help himself. He'd tried to be so strong for me and we had just had the perfect week together, carrying on as we always had. But, exactly a week from then, would be the start of my treatment process. I faced the day in theatre, the fear of not waking from the anaesthetic, and not really knowing what the future held.

When we arrived home, I made sure I kept myself really busy. I spring cleaned a dozen times over - a typical scenario of obsessive compulsive disorder taking control. I made sure all the bedding was washed; every kitchen cupboard cleaned out; every wardrobe tidied and all clothes sorted. I had a production line going in the kitchen as I spent hours cooking. The freezer was packed with casseroles; Bolognaise sauce, lasagne, curry, and cottage pie. I needed to know that, whilst I was in hospital, Giles was eating well; I still wanted to look after him and didn't want him to worry about anything. I was intent in making sure the house was tidy and looked as homely as I could make it with all the feminine touches in place, just in case. I even went to see one of Giles' friends who I knew really well and trusted. I wanted him to promise me he would look after Giles and the girls if anything happened to me. He thought I was slightly crazy and told me, "Sarah, you're going to be fine. Nothing is going to happen to you, so stop worrying." He gave me a cuddle. I knew I had to do all those things in preparation. I even wrote a note and put it in my jewellery box telling which piece of jewellery would go to whom.

The evening before my operation, I drove the girls to my mum and dads' house, with their little suitcases I'd methodically packed. They stayed there whilst I was in hospital. Leaving them was one of my saddest moments as I felt drained – depressed and beaten. I didn't stay long before I kissed them and gave them a massive hug- told them how much I loved them. Little did they know what I was just about to go through the next day. Then I hugged mum and dad as they told me that they would be thinking of me all day and I got in my car and drove home. I couldn't look back. Tears streamed down my face. I sobbed uncontrollably. My thoughts were engulfed: how would they all react if anything happened to me - paranoid that something would happen under the anaesthetic.

20

Farewell left breast

I was up at about four o'clock in the morning, after a long lonely night of sleeplessness. I tossed and turned and worried I had everything in order, as I watched the clock, desperate, oddly enough, for it to strike the next hour. I waited as long as I could before I got up and ran a piping hot bath, a different scene than just lying in bed, but the same worries going through my mind. I lay in the bath staring at my body, stroking my chest as I said my farewell, it didn't feel it belonged to me anymore, though, almost as if my brain had disconnected all feelings in order to protect myself. My stomach churned, I had butterflies as I lay there feeling sick, anxious and nervous. But I lay there for as long as I could, I looked like a prune, making the most of not being able to have a bath for a good couple of weeks. Giles got up and made us both a cup of tea, in a world of his own, forgetting I wasn't allowed to have anything to drink. I got myself dressed and ready, the house feeling so empty and quiet without the kids being at home. I walked into their bedrooms and straightened up the teddy's on their beds to make sure everything looked perfect before setting off for hospital.

As I got in the car I stared up at our house, the home I was building, and silently thought that I hoped to come back to it in a few days. Then we made our way to hospital in virtual silence, apart from the occasional "Sars you going to be fine, I promise you" and a gentle squeeze of my hand, a sign that we were going through this together. I was incoherent, distracted in my own world, and couldn't communicate. I needed to prepare myself for what was about to come and I wanted to do this alone which meant blocking Giles out. We had left home a little bit too early and sat in the hospital foyer for a few minutes, engrossed in our own thoughts, before we made our way up to the admissions ward. Immediately we were taken into a small room with a bed and two chairs and I was given a sexy hospital gown to put on as all the paper work was completed and my name tags in place.

The first person who came to see me was the registrar assisting Mr Schreuder that day. I really can't remember what he said to me but strangely enough I remember he wore beige cords and a red checked shirt! Then Mr Schreuder arrived shortly afterwards, followed by the breast surgeon from Bedford Hospital. I remember Mr Schreuder sitting down to talk to me while everyone else stood over me. They asked me if I had any questions, but I was so emotional I couldn't talk. I was like a terrified rabbit wanting them to just get on with it, the waiting was killing me. I could sense that they felt that my attitude was slightly strange but I don't think they understood quite how anxious I was. I was absolutely petrified particularly when the big black marker pen came out with all its vapours and they started to draw the outlines where all my scars would be, a big eye shape was drawn on my chest with arrows confirming the lump area coupled with a mark from one hip bone to the other. Although I did manage a nervous smile when they mentioned that the small freckle I had just on my ribs would feature right at the bottom of my tummy when I woke up. My skin stretched that much.

Giles walked me down to the theatre floor and to an ante-room before the anaesthetic room. I couldn't help but notice that the theatres were right next to the hospital chapel and that is the last thing I saw before I went into the theatre area. The nurse's double checked my identity. I cried yet again. Saying goodbye to Giles was awful. "I love you so much" were the last words I spoke to him before the operation. The anaesthetist was great. "Why are you crying? You're going to be fine" he said whilst handing me some tissues. They obviously get that reaction all of the time. I was shaking

"Hey, I promise you I won't let anything happen to you because if it does I won't get paid, and I can't afford for that to happen." Funny how I remember his exact words but not those of the consultants upstairs, apart from the freckle.

"You'll be fine, I'll look after you," he said as he wheeled me into the anaesthetic room. He had a very calming influence on me and kept talking to me whilst he attempted to stick needles into me. I was all ready for the anaesthetic and that was it. I was out and I never did get asked to count down from ten.

Hurray. I woke up in the recovery room. A huge sense of relief. But I was freezing cold and shaking. I remember I felt tense and sore, but I couldn't have done. I would have been pumped with so many painkillers. As soon as I was stabilised, I was wheeled up to the ward, 11B by a porter and nurse. I have to say those night porters are inconsiderate drivers when it comes to wheeling those beds - banging into walls on the way and going fast over the little grids into the lift, four bumps you might find that is, and when you've just had surgery, that hurts! When you have a 'free tram DIEP flap' you are kept in a tropical environment. My room was uncomfortable and terribly hot to allow the flap to take. The high temperature helps to ensure a healthy blood flow reaches the donor tissue. If there was an insufficient blood supply that tissue would die. I knew that I had to remain in that climate for roughly three days with the sweat pouring from me. I had a line in me which allowed me to administer my own pain relief when I needed it. I had morphine available at the press of a pump whenever needed. I remember Giles being in my room when I got there and then Mr Schreuder and his registrar came in to tell us, or Giles, that the operation had been successful and had gone very well but had taken a little longer than anticipated. I was incredibly drowsy and every twinge I felt I pressed the morphine pump. I was so relieved to see Giles' little face waiting for me, but far too drowsy to engage in any conversation with him. I slept the entire night, oblivious to being monitored every half an hour, and all through the following day, only managing to press the morphine pump whenever I felt a slight twinge. By the Friday morning I was delirious and Giles was really concerned. I overheard the surgeons as they told him that I would be absolutely fine. I felt nauseous. I could only groan to myself to try and make myself feel better. Then it dawned on me that maybe I was being a little too trigger happy with the pain relief and for the rest of the morning refrained from pressing it. By lunchtime, I felt so much brighter and actually managed to have a drink and something to eat. Fish and chips - it was Friday. I have given that bit of advice to a friend who also had breast surgery. "Whatever you do don't press that morphine pump because it will make you feel sick." When Giles returned in the evening he couldn't believe the improvement in me and was so delighted to have me back in the world of the living.

I was still very sore and not ready to take the almighty step of trying to get myself up and out of bed. The nursing staff try and encourage you to get up and walk around as soon as possible but I think your body tells you when you are ready, and my body was telling me to leave it to the following day – Saturday. I knew that my girls would be coming in then with my mum and dad and thought that it would be great for them to see me up and walking around when they came. To be perfectly honest, although it was relatively painful to get myself sitting up and out of bed, it was certainly no more painful than having a Caesarean. What was apparent though was how my chest felt as though it had an enormous concrete slab attached to it. It was just so heavy and tight, even more so when standing up. I hadn't had the confidence to take a peep at what my new breast looked like. Even though I had been woken up constantly through the day and night by the nurses ensuring that that the flap looked healthy, I always looked away at that stage. I could only take one step at a time and I wasn't quite ready to see the big change to the appearance of my body. I needed to grow accustomed to it first all in my own time.

Rather like childbirth the hormones kicked in four days later and the emotions of the last few weeks touched home. I cried buckets! This was coupled with me peeping at just a little of my new breast, which, I am ashamed to say, looked the most disgusting thing I had ever seen. It was all swollen and bruised and even seemed to have a strange aroma to it. My heart just sank and I felt totally dejected. One of the nurses saw me crying and came in to comfort and talk to me. I felt so ungrateful. I hated my reconstruction. I didn't like what it looked like. I certainly didn't like what it felt like. Shortly after my chat with the nurse, the registrar came to see me whilst on his ward round. He was aware of how I felt already and just sat on the end of the bed and made his speech.

"Don't get down. You're really lucky to have had the type of reconstruction. It's the best procedure currently available and you should be feeling really proud of what has been done for you. Take a moment to go and have a proper look at the breast and feel really comfortable when doing this. We won't be able to send you home until you fully accept the surgery."

He told me how lucky I was that the cancer had been caught in the early stages. My initial reaction was, *typical man, what do you know about being thirty six years of age and having your breast removed? How can you ever understand?* But oh how I hear his words echo so strongly with me now!

Giles came to see me later that morning. He knew I felt low and gave me a massive cuddle. He arrived with a full bowl of juicy fresh fruit mum had peeled and prepared. She knows I don't eat oranges unless someone peels them for me. Then I really enjoy them. Although I think Giles thought she had done this for his benefit as he freely tucked straight into them and asked me if I fancied any!

"Do you want to have a proper look at my breast?" I courageously asked him. With the door closed I showed him, but looked away myself.

"That's fantastic. I can't believe how wonderful it is, I'm really surprised how neat all the scarring is. It's brilliant." Wow. He could see beyond the swelling and bruising.

"Do you think it's that good?"

"It's brilliant Sarah." That gave me the comfort to have a closer look later on. I was still not convinced that it was 'brilliant', but perhaps that was due to it feeling so unnatural and heavy. The registrar came in to double check on me later on.

"How are you feeling now? Have you had a chance to have a proper look? Are you happy with the look?"

"I'm feeling better. It looks great. I was just feeling emotional this morning," I lied, but I wasn't going to risk not going home.

"We'll see about getting you discharged tomorrow then."

"Wow, that soon" I remarked with sudden trepidation. I think they tend to like you out of hospital as quickly as possible to prevent any infections.

I was discharged, five days after my twelve hour operation, which is incredible. I opted to go home to mum and dad's so I could be looked after by mum, but have the girls around me with all their needs taken care of by mum as well. I was really sore. My stomach constantly stung. Getting in and out of bed was painful. I hated not being able to do anything or have a bath. Each time I got up I thought my stomach was going to drop out of me and my boob was going to drop off. My chest felt as though it was burning with all the tissue knitting together. I was in for a much slower recovery than I anticipated. I didn't feel I was healing. I had a small breakdown of tissue in my stomach that was slow to heal. It was like a little hole which I could have poked a pencil into - almost like a pencil sharpener and I made lots of trips to the clinic to have all the dressing changed and the hole packed with silver until it was healed completely. It was at mums as the days passed that I came to accept my reconstructed breast, even forgetting where I was one day and showing my dad how brilliant it was.

"Isn't the surgeon an incredible man?" I said.

"It's marvellous when you see what they can do," dad said.

I had my six week follow up appointment with Mr Schreuder in clinic and he was really pleased with how I was getting on. Sometimes in life it's easier to say "I'm fine thank you" when someone asks how you are feeling. I told him how pleased I was with how everything had gone. Deep down this wasn't quite true. I felt as though I had really struggled to get over my operation. The recovery and healing had been slow and there appeared to still be quite a significant amount of swelling, too. I also had a huge mass of area that had absolutely no feeling at all. I'm sure that he actually thought that I had sailed through the whole procedure and recovery process and that I was really happy with the result. There was still an area of breakdown – an open wound on my breast, which needed to heal so we made another appointment for me to see him again in six weeks.

21

Results

Three weeks after my surgery I returned to the Primrose Unit for my results and to go through the next course of treatment. Giles was with me on this occasion, especially after my initial appointment with the oncologist had left me plagued with uncertainty. We were so nervous in case we received bad news. We were called into the oncologist's consulting room and, as previously, were left to wait again until he was ready to see us. I don't know why he did this. Why didn't he just call me through when he was ready to see us?

"Do you realise how off putting and unnerving it is when you are a patient, a worried and anxious one at that, to be kept waiting in this little room on our own? Do you understand what we are going through?" I asked him, when he made his appearance.

"I am sorry. I was just getting the rest of your results from the Lister as I didn't have them. How are you feeling anyway after your surgery?" Gosh, he was human, but always very matter of fact. He sat down to run through the reports that had detained him.

"The tumour was 2.5cm and it was in one of the four nodes that we removed, which makes it node positive at stage two. You are triple negative which means that it will not respond to any hormone replacement treatment after the chemo. I am going to give you eight sessions of chemotherapy and this will be administered every three weeks."

He repeated the type of cancer I had was the kind that affects younger people, and there was a strong possibility its cause was my previous radiotherapy. I was surprised at the amount of chemo he suggested but I could sense for the first time that he wanted to do his best for me.

"So triple negative breast cancer - is that a good one to get?" I asked.

"You'll be fine" he said. I didn't want to be told any more.

He was not in a position to proceed with the chemo-therapy as I had not healed properly. Chemotherapy would knock my whole immune system and the areas not healed would then be at great risk of infections, so he advised that we waited another four weeks.

22

So which is the real size 36?

My breast surgeon really cheered me up when I saw him next in my follow up appointment.

"I'm really pleased with how things have gone for you - the reconstruction is the best I have seen."

"Really?" I replied, "That makes me feel an awful lot better."

He had a young training doctor with him. "So tell me which one do you think has had the reconstruction then?" he asked. The young doctor just looked at my chest and paused. I did have to smile. It really wasn't that difficult a question to answer as one clearly didn't have a nipple on it! I wonder if he ever made it.

The consultant then took a more serious tone.

"Now Sarah, because you have tested node positive to the disease, we want to give you the best treatment so you can get on with your life. But I think that it will be in your best interest if we go ahead and do the axillary clearance at the end of your chemo, just to be on the safe side," he advised.

"How long will that operation take?" was the first question that came into my mind.

"About one and a half to two hours."

"Oh, so a piece of cake then. Can this be done under a local anaesthetic or do I have to be put to sleep?"

Unfortunately it was the latter since axillary clearance involved removing all of the lymph nodes from under my arm.

23

Chemotherapy: Fec - it's awful

Eight weeks after my surgery date my chemotherapy started. It is very hard to find the words that describe the Primrose Unit. My original impression had changed as I became more familiar with the environment and staff. It was a relatively new unit that felt so calm, peaceful and quiet to walk into. The receptionists always greeted you with a smile. "Hello Sarah" they would say before I got to the desk, "how are you today, just take a seat and you will be called through shortly." I often wondered if they had been trained to have such caring, compassionate voices without actually sounding condescending.

What was very apparent when I sat down and looked around was just how dressed up I was – dressed up and made up. I made sure I wore clothes that were bright and cheerful looking to make me feel more positive and help portray a gleaming picture of health, and my smile was a deliberate attempt to hide the realistic fact – I felt incredibly frightened. I was about to experience the awful, unpleasant side effects of my chemotherapy treatment. Looking around the waiting room I noted the people around me had decades on me. I was the oddity, the young one who everyone could easily mistake as the family member or friend accompanying a loved one for that particular chemo session.

I was quickly called through to the chemo suite. The first time I looked in the suite was when I had my first appointment with my oncologist and I found it so frightening and difficult to comprehend that one day I would be sitting in one of the large old-fashioned armchairs to receive my treatment. They reminded me of the day room in the care home that my Nan lived in for the last couple of years of her life. Now the day had come for my treatment to start and I was left having to make a decision. Which vacant armchair looked the most comfortable – we would be there for some time. In true Giles style we opted for one right in the middle of the suite, in the midst of all the comings and goings! As we sat down I reached for Giles' hand, desperate for that reassurance that I was going to be ok and that he would take care of me. We spoke very quietly to each other as he tried to make the situation light hearted. I glanced around the suite and noticed how poorly some patients looked. I honestly felt I didn't belong there in my pink lipstick and blusher and bright pink jumper with the sleeve rolled up over my elbow waiting in anticipation for the cannula insertion, the tiny tube that would sit in my vein.

I was quite nervous of my chemo nurse to begin with. From a distance she always seemed to frown as she peered over the top of her little half glasses that were attached to a chain around her neck. She looked like a headmistress, very authoritative and she shouted at me when she saw me cross my legs. "You'll get varicose veins" frowning as she told me off. However, when she came to put the cannula in my hand it became very apparent just how friendly, reassuring, positive and realistic she was. Her name is Laurie and I still think of her today but I know that she has now moved away from the area.

My veins have always been a nightmare. They were very tiny and extremely difficult to put a needle in. Every nurse or doctor struggled to find them, and they certainly liked to go into hiding particularly when it came to having toxic juice. It took at least forty five minutes to successfully put the needle into my veins in the back of my hand after being punctured a few times further up my arm. Even that was after I had sat with a warm lavender bag over my arm trying to coax my veins to make an appearance before placing my arm in a sink of hot water to get the veins to surface. It was only then that they were ready to be injected with that really toxic liquid that swam its way through those finally plumped up veins. Was it any wonder that they didn't want to introduce themselves?

My first four sessions of chemotherapy consisted of being given FEC. FEC was named after the initials of the chemotherapy drugs used and I really don't want to bore you with details of them and secondly I don't know how to spell them. I had to wait a while for these drugs to be made up and delivered from the pharmacy. They needed to be concocted and administered within a tight time frame - if not, they were thrown away.

I always arrived at the hospital looking the picture of health in my entire make up to look human and feminine but I really didn't know why I bothered. I was quickly given the first drug which within seconds stripped me of my public dignity and made me feel like I'd sat naked in a field of nettles and all I wanted to do was have a good old scratch at my nether regions to relieve me of the intense stinging that took me completely by surprise. I knew those pelvic floor exercises would come in handy one day as I squeezed tightly to try and alleviate the unpleasant discomfort, which actually only lasted a matter of seconds.

"What were these drugs made up of to have that instant a reaction?" I laughed at Laurie, when the sensation faded, "...I wasn't expecting that!"

Then it was syringe number two. A nice big fat juicy syringe filled with a beautiful bright red liquid. On the first visit to the toilet afterwards your wee showed up bright red, too! They didn't tell me that! The anti sickness drugs delivered with the chemotherapy immediately made me feel incredibly drowsy. I tended to fall asleep for a couple of hours while the nurse continued injecting the remaining drugs. Giles was always with me so he was the one who sat there talking to the nurses whilst I fell asleep with my mouth wide open, dribbling in a manner which must have looked very unrefined. I had my chemotherapy as a day patient so, as soon as my cannula was removed, I was free to go home and continue to sleep it all off. I had anti-sickness tablets to take home. I was told to make sure that I took them, even if I did not feel sick, as the drugs were much better at preventing sickness rather than stopping it once started. Then all I had to do was wait and see how my body coped and reacted to those foreign highly toxic drugs that were making their way through my body, killing off the enemy.

I had a clockwork routine at home. The evening before my chemotherapy treatment without fail I always made a cottage pie for dinner for the following evening so all Giles needed to do when we got home was cook some prepared broccoli and carrots and warm the cottage pie for the girls. It was important during this period that the girls had a healthy, wholesome diet as well to help keep the colds and bugs at bay as much as possible.

When I had chemotherapy part of my treatment was a course of steroids, too, which actually gave me mood swings for a short period. I would take the steroids, which were in tablet form, the day before my next course of chemotherapy. One particular morning I had taken my steroids when I decided that I needed to get my ironing up to date before I went off to hospital. I only had a couple of shirts to iron for Giles so I got the ironing board out, put it up, plugged the iron in and just as I was about to start ironing, a little voice piped up, "… don't worry about doing that, I can do it when we get home from hospital."

Imagine my interpretation: "You are so ungrateful for everything that I do for you" as the ironing board flew across the kitchen. Then a hurl of abuse as I told him "…you don't have to bother taking me to hospital. I'm quite capable of getting on a bus." I flung on my coat and flounced to the High Street bus stop. I waited. I didn't know the bus time-table. The steroid induced anger was fading. I hoped Giles would just drive by and pick me up – and he did.

We always arrived in the chemo suite united and full of smiles and chat – on this occasion, the events of the previous hour forgotten - and often delivered a cake or biscuits for the nurses - a small token of our appreciation as they did such a wonderful job and it must have been really difficult and traumatic for them at times. The Primrose Unit became a place where I quickly felt safe and became quite institutionalised in a good sense. I no longer looked apart. We were united by ordeal, and, in the case of the staff, to help deal with it to the best of their ability. I felt secure in the knowledge that these special people were doing everything in their power to make me better.

I was lucky. My first couple of doses of chemotherapy didn't really make me feel very ill. The anti-sickness drugs worked. I did feel very nauseous but I wasn't physically sick. Just as well because if you knew me you would quickly realise that I don't handle vomit very well! I seemed to cope with what I was dealt quite remarkably. I was very tired for a week after chemo but that seemed to be the only side effect that I suffered during that time. But it was bad enough: chemo tiredness is completely different. You could sleep for hours without feeling a benefit. It's debilitating, a feeling to be associated with rigorous medical treatment.

24

Vein to vanity

So chemotherapy went as well as it could, until two weeks after my second course I was faced with what I'm sure all woman dread. As I sat in my study working (I'm fortunate to work from home), I started to run my fingers through my hair when it just came away in clumps. I didn't feel anything at all, and I knew that it was the right time to do the radical thing. I couldn't bear to shave my head myself as that meant that I would have to look in the mirror. I was not ready to face that. Instead, I plucked up the courage and phoned my friend Deborah, who came straight round with her clippers and shaved the rest of my hair off in the kitchen for me. So there I stood with my big round pudding face with nothing to frame it. Now I truly looked like a victim of cancer. The first time I looked in the mirror I noticed how round my face was. I've always been blessed with high cheek bones, but I looked more puffy than usual and I had developed dark puffy circles under my eyes caused from the lack of sleep. I looked shorter and fatter for some reason. I had prepared myself mentally for losing my hair so I didn't cry, at least not initially. Instead I walked straight upstairs and placed my wig on and reapplied my lipstick. I'd had fun with Deborah shopping for a wig and I'd had it for some time. I tried every imaginable style. Some made me look ten years older before I decided on the one I chose. But when I put it on this time and for a purpose I almost felt like I had become a different person in my body instantly and that I was as light as a feather as I floated above myself trying to make a connection between me and the figure I saw before me in the mirror. I'd almost detached myself from within to protect myself.

From that moment on I always wore my lovely long wig for the next few months, and I had a little bobble hat for the evenings to relax in and keep my head warm. You don't realise how much warmth you lose through your head until you haven't got any hair! I opted for a long wig as I always wished for long hair. But instead I was blessed with fine hair that I was never able to grow longer than my shoulders and look decent. I figured that everyone that I knew was aware it was a wig anyway so I may as well just go for it. When I wore my wig the first time and collected Annabel from school she told me I looked like a Barbie in it. I never knew if I should have taken that as a compliment or not, but knowing Annabel it would no doubt be the latter!

I felt you can hide the illness when all you have to undergo is surgery, but you couldn't hide it when physical

changes happen to you. Naturally I was quite self conscious; I didn't feel comfortable wearing a head scarf as
it really wasn't me. I didn't mind people who knew me
knowing what I had, but to the outside world I wanted to
appear completely normal. Bizarre really, I suppose, after
all I wasn't really in control of what was happening to me.

My third course of chemotherapy was definitely the
most horrific. As soon as I got home from hospital I was
sick constantly. No sooner had I taken my anti-sickness
tablets they came back up again. I felt terrible. I leant over
the toilet during the night trying to subdue the sounds of
my violent retching, so as not to disturb the children. My
whole body shaking and shivering and I was hot and cold.
I felt faint, had cold sweats which made me roll around
on the bathroom floor. I had to ride it to get through it.
As the days rolled on my whole body ached through to
my bones making me feel even fainter and my fingers
and toes tingled. All I could do was sway and moan and
rock myself. Then the stomach cramps started, followed
by awful bouts of diarrhoea which doubled me up in
agony; I suffered some of the most humiliating moments
as the girls watched me struggle at being caught short
before managing to get anywhere near the toilet. I often
cried, sometimes so embarrassed that my children were
witness to this and feeling that it was just so unfair. All I
wanted to do was crawl back into bed and sleep my way
through it all. I was so tired. But chemotherapy and cancer
chooses the rules of the game. Instead it decided to send

my mind into overdrive when I should have been fast asleep making me so irrational. I had bursts of all kinds of negative thoughts as soon as I closed my eyes. The aches and pains were no longer side effects of treatment but the cancer taking hold and targeting my bones. I would cry quietly as Giles slept beside me, so he couldn't hear me thinking that this was it and the chemo wasn't working. He'd always wake when I needed to blow my nose. I was so terribly tired and devoid of all energy. I didn't even manage to walk downstairs. I was only on round three and I still had five to go. What was I going to feel like by the end? My chemo nurse called me at the end of that week to ensure I was alright. Perhaps most patients suffered on that dose. I became so accustomed to feeling exhausted it felt normal.

After four sessions of chemo the drugs were changed for the final four rounds and I reduced to only one drug which was again given intravenously. I was always drowsy as soon as I was given it and it took a good couple of hours to inject. But now I knew the whole routine: go home, put pyjamas on and sleep it all off for a few hours; and then be wide awake for the rest of the night, emotionally and physically shattered. In the morning I pushed myself really hard to get myself out of bed as I needed to make the packed lunches and take the children to school. I had lots of friends offering to take the children but I was determined to do it myself; it gave me the focus I needed. By the time I reached the end of chemo I felt exhausted, breathless and found it tough to exert myself in even the smallest way. The fatigue was the most constant side effect that I had to deal with and it got progressively worse as the months moved on. I did work throughout my treatment because I felt I needed to occupy myself but I got as much rest as I could whenever I had the opportunity. Although I didn't really feel like it I was told to get a little bit of gentle exercise like walking to try to boost my energy levels... "just a slow paced walk - nothing strenuous."

Unfortunately chemotherapy doesn't just attack cancerous cells in your body. It also attacks and destroys healthy cells in the process. My blood count dropped dramatically, leaving me quite vulnerable to all sorts of infections. It is important to try to maintain a healthy diet during this period to fight these infections: lots of fruit and vegetables rich in iron and plenty of protein. Clearly there are times when you just have to have what you fancy. I don't believe in taking vitamin supplements as I think that you should get all of these from eating a varied well balanced diet and drinking lots of water to flush out the toxins that the drugs cause.

When I had my chemo, no matter how battered I felt, I always planned something to really look forward to and it really made the time fly by between treatments. Afternoon tea with friends, a night at the theatre, or simply meeting a friend for a coffee in Starbucks meant that I had to get myself up and ready. I felt it was so important not to just lie there and play the victim, which we can all be guilty of at some stage, and I wanted to be better than that. A positive mind is a priceless asset, believe me.

On my last appointment with my oncologist just before my final session of chemo I had to ask a question that I wanted to ask six months earlier, but I could only deal with one thing at a time. When the analysis had come back from the laboratory when I had had my mastectomy, the oncologist mentioned that the cancer may have been caused by the radiotherapy previously given. I had received radiotherapy to the whole of my chest area. So surely the right side of my chest would be at risk of developing breast cancer also. I needed to ask if it would be advisable to go ahead with surgery to this side as well. It transpired my oncologist was thinking along the same lines. In order for me to make a decision he referred me to a breast care specialist at Addenbrooke's Hospital in Cambridge, who also had experience of dealing with Hodgkin's disease patients.

To celebrate the end of my chemo and toast my impending birthday, I invited ten girl friends to a local Chinese restaurant to mark the occasion. Everyone met at our house and Giles served us all pink champagne - sorry it wasn't topless male waiters, I couldn't afford them - and Olivia and Annabel put their fine waitressing skills to the test and offered canapés. Everyone bought me a little pink gift as a token for what I had been through, which really touched me and I really felt I should say a little thank you and a few words, but I was actually speechless. I didn't feel comfortable speaking in front of the girls. I didn't want to alarm them or for them to sense that something serious had been wrong. So the first thought that came into my mind was, "It's not all that bad really." As the evening developed and copious amounts of wine drunk, even by me - and I hadn't had a proper drink for a few months - I became rather loose tongued. I decided to tell a little story about the very initial thing that I noticed when I first looked at my new boob which really put me off it. "The very first time I took a proper look at my new boob I noticed seven pubic hairs protruded on my chest." The table burst into hysterical giggles as I went on "…I couldn't believe that Mr Schreuder had the whole vast area of my stomach to choose from and lo and behold he had chosen the skin well below my belly button with these added little hairs."

Not very attractive I know but just my luck I thought. Thanks Fred!

Thankfully I have taken care of those now, but they were the last thing that I ever thought I would wake up to. To this day this story still provides huge amusement especially when the men are on the scene having a few beers and wine. Even if I have become a target for teasing I'm really lucky to have these people around me to restore the humour in something that alternatively is quite horrific and almost taboo.

When I was told that I would have eight sessions of chemo which would last six months, I expected that time to feel like a lifetime, waiting and dreading those diary dates. Looking back on them they almost passed in an instant and before I knew it, I'd done it. Thankfully it was all over. I thought I would feel relieved, excited, and so happy that it was over so that I could leave it behind me but I didn't. I felt incredibly low and depressed, stripped of everything that defined me of what I was, a woman. I sat in the evening, adamant that I didn't want to go out, be with other woman, with their clothes, hair and makeup in place just making me feel more isolated and uncomfortable in my skin. Instead I wanted to stay in, put my bobble hat on and lock the door. I had few eyebrows to frame my eyes and little broken off eyelashes that I attempted to put mascara on but just ended up with blobs instead. My body was scarred with vast areas of numbness and little sensation. The girls would sit beside me and innocently tell me how 'cute' I looked.

"Ah mummy," they would coo beside me. I was still just their mummy to them. I hadn't changed at all and that was the comfort that I sought. It took a great, strong man to stand beside me and tell me how much he loved me even though he had watched me stripped of all dignity, doing things for me that we would have expected when we are in our eighties, I didn't think I could ever look feminine again. We may have had our love for each other seriously tested but I know that I have a very special person by my side forever. Nothing will ever take that away from me!

25

Hollow arm pit

Six weeks after my chemotherapy ended, I revisited my breast consultant to discuss the final stage of my surgery with him - the axillary clearance. Despite having an air of authority about him, I liked him. He'd been part of the team that saved my life. I related to him and felt he was human because he had a really dry sense of humour and I actually found him amusing. Sarcasm may have been better but any sense of humour was welcome at the time. I needed to have the axillary clearance as my cancer had spread to the sentinel node and having the clearance reduced the chances of any stray cell spreading through my body. The clearance involved removing all of the lymph nodes from under my arm. I couldn't have radiation treatment so the clearance was the only alternative measure. However, it left me with the risk of developing lymphoedema for the rest of my life. (I actually developed it three years later as I had no lymphatic drainage system on the left hand side of my body. My lymphatic system had been so compromised it was inevitable that I was going to be prone to swelling caused by lymph fluid building up. My body didn't have a system in place to drain it away.) I acted on the advice given to go ahead with surgery to ensure I gave myself the best possible treatment and chance to get on with the rest of my life.

On the morning of surgery I was remarkably calm, although my biggest concern bizarrely was how I looked. My hair had started to grow back slightly but nowhere near enough to show it off to the public. Lianne, my friend and 'rock' through my treatment, had kept laughing at me when I told her I wasn't looking forward to being wheeled into theatre. I wouldn't be able to wear my wig and I didn't want anyone to see me and know that I had been ill. Most people thought that would be the absolute least of all my worries.

When I arrived on the ward I was immediately shown to my bed. It was the first time I had been in Bedford Hospital for any length since having my children. I observed how spotless and clean that surgical ward was and how the nurses appeared jolly and happy, too, which instantly allowed me to feel at ease. I knew that I didn't need to watch the toilet like a hawk and hit it as soon as it had been cleaned and I felt comfortable. My breast surgeon came to see me prior to surgery and explained what he would be doing in theatre and marked me up. He was always so matter of fact, but I trusted him.

"So how big do you think the scar will be then?" I asked him.

He just looked at me with a really baffled expression on his face as he began to show me with his hands.

"Wow that big?" I sounded alarmed.

"It's a scar," he said, "the least of your worries."

I laughed. I suppose with hindsight this was very true.

I stayed in hospital for a week following the operation and I was surprised by how much agony I was in. I remember it was painful to move my arm or raise it. I had no idea it would be that sore, - getting dressed was impossible, as was raising a fork to eat. My arm was numb from my shoulder to my elbow and quite swollen. I dreaded getting lymphoedema. I didn't want to look like one of those old ladies, looking like I had elephantiasis. Thankfully the swelling subsided. What the hospital failed to advise was the condition was manageable with correct treatment and massage, so I worried unnecessarily for a period. My scar, I'm happy to say, was a very neat little line which was so faint I could hardly see it even when it was new. Although what I hadn't realised was how my underarm looked as though it had a big ball of pastry dough removed from it.

When I had any of my surgery I was also given lots of information on the best exercises that I needed to do daily to retain maximum flexibility. I religiously performed them ensuring I escaped from any loss of movement.

When I had my six week follow up appointment with my breast surgeon he was delighted with the healing and lack of swelling and I was overjoyed with the tiny faint scar that he had left me with.

"You didn't tell me my arm would feel that painful" I told him, making him laugh.

"I understand you are going to go to Addenbrooke's Hospital in Cambridge to see a specialist regarding a second mastectomy," he quizzed me. My notes were always kept up to date.

"Yes, a second opinion I suppose," I answered. "What are your thoughts?"

"In my experience I think it would be unlikely to get a recurrence in the second breast and I don't really see it being a concern in the future," he paused before adding, "... but naturally this isn't a guarantee and we are unable to say for certain."

That was almost confirmation for my gut feeling, as he said "I'm prepared for you to go ahead with the appointment to help you make your decision."

I didn't challenge the opinion but I felt I was being regarded solely as a breast cancer patient, not as a breast cancer patient that had survived Hodgkin's disease. Thankfully I kept myself well informed of my medical past.

26

Planting the seed

My appointment in the plastic surgery department followed a few days after my discussion with my breast consultant. This follow-up appointment was to discuss the nipple reconstruction and to make the adjustment to the outer fullness of this new breast. I saw the registrar who assisted Mr Schreuder in theatre with my reconstruction. I was pleased to see him as it made me feel like I had great continuity in my care. As he read my records he noted I was exploring further preventative surgery to the other breast.

"Obviously you have already had reconstructive surgery on one side," he began, "so I presume if you decide to go down this road you will decide to have a second reconstruction?"

"Naturally I suppose a second reconstruction makes perfect sense." I replied tentatively. I had only thought as far as getting a second opinion. I couldn't mentally tackle further surgery until after the Addenbrooke's consultation had taken place.

"As you have already had surgery on your stomach it means that this area of your body is no longer an option to use as a donor site," he advised. I already knew that I could not use my back due to the level of radiotherapy I have had. "…the best option you are left with is your buttock," the registrar continued. "Due to the nature of this procedure Mr Schreuder would not be able to perform this surgery. He has never performed this complex procedure before, but there is a surgeon who has pioneered this procedure which is called an I gap (inferior gluteal artery perforator). It involves removing skin, fat and muscle from your lower buttock and we would be more than happy to refer you on."

My world started to close in on me. I didn't want to go anywhere else, leaving behind a team of people that had woken me from one lengthy operation, and left me with a reconstruction that I was finally beginning to love. On that note Mr Schreuder came into the consulting room and when briefed on our conversation by the registrar looked at me with a concerned expression and sat down.

"Please don't worry. Go and have your discussion in Cambridge and when you have made your decision telephone my secretary, Helen, and let her know the outcome before you come back to see me in three months time," he said. He was sympathetic but he also went on to advise: "…I must let you know that the Igap procedure will be another lengthy procedure, between ten to twelve hours." He probably read my anxiety. "If you decide not to go

126

ahead with the second mastectomy, I will lift your natural breast to match the other one and give you the cleavage of a twenty year old." He said trying to lighten the mood.

How could that not raise a smile from me? But through that smile, he could sense my apprehension and we ended the appointment on that note.

I had absorbed as much advice as I could, but as I left the hospital my overriding concern was slightly irrational – the surgeon I most trusted would not be performing the next operation if it took place.

27

Body language speaks volumes

Giles took the afternoon off work to accompany me to Addenbrooke's to see a leading breast care specialist. I would never have found my way there on my own: the hospital is enormous; even the roads around it confused me. I would definitely have got stressed prior to my appointment - worrying that I would be late. "Have you got a list of all the questions you want to ask? It's important to get them all answered today," he reminded me as we were parking the car.

My reasons for the referral were to establish the risk of recurrence. I was advised the specialist had treated lots of Hodgkin's disease patients in her time and I wanted to know what decisions those patients had made regarding the heightened susceptibility we shared.

The oncology department was huge. It is the main specialist cancer unit regionally and the oncologists in Bedford work under the instruction of the hospital, sharing knowledge and information. I felt completely out of my own comfort zone in terms of being amongst a medical team of people who knew me, and a team of whom I was growing fond and felt at ease in their presence. I was called through by the specialist. With shoulder length brown hair and glasses, she appeared very aloof, and very direct in her approach. At my local hospitals, I was treated very well, the entire team had been exceptionally positive with my progress and outcome. I had really grown to love them. They were my font of knowledge as I chose not to read any literature or do any research on my type of breast cancer and they had the intuition to understand how much I could deal with at any one time. I remained under their care as naive as I could. I can understand it's sometimes necessary to be scientifically objective and to leave the empathy to more immediate medical teams. The new Cambridge specialist frightened me on two fronts. I was there to obtain as much information as I could and just watched as she started reading my files.

"Mm..." That brief utterance alerted me in the first instance to negativity. I had learnt how to read body language extremely well and to interpret the way in which news was delivered. Perception of what is unsaid as much as what is said is issued with the hospital bed. "You had triple negative breast cancer," she confirmed, her tone giving me the impression that this wasn't the best form to be blessed with; and I was too scared to actually ask her what this meant in terms of the nature of the disease. Instead I swiftly asked what I had gone to discover. " So out of all of the Hodgkin's disease patients you have treated, what did they all do in relation to having a double mastectomy?" Her answer still haunts me to this day and it doesn't matter how enormously positive I may be or how I must believe that the future is bright, I certainly wasn't prepared for her answer, "None of them made it." As clear as crystal I still hear her say those words to me even now – although, what is very curious, is that Giles doesn't recall them at all, and he sat beside me at the time. The specialist's words rang an alarm. When you live with cancer, you have a personal, and stridently alert, perception and interpretation of every nuance. I'm scared that it could strike again. Only next time it could be more aggressive.

For a moment she flummoxed me, almost making me lose focus on the single issue I wanted answered. She had caught me off guard and I was unprepared for her gloomy patient statistics. At the same time, I felt if I cried she would regard me as being pathetic. I tried really hard to control my welling tears. My voice broke. As I spoke to her my throat dried but I pushed on with the vital question.

"So what would you do if you were me then? Would you go ahead and have the surgery?" Trying to read a reaction, a small smile in my mind confirmed my gut feeling. I do know that a medical professional is not allowed to tell you what to do; you must make all the decisions, based on your own researches, questions, experience and instincts. If I wanted to go ahead with surgery my medical records and history needed to be referred to an independent team of surgeons and oncologists at Addenbrooke's to see whether my request could be justified. They would make the final decision.

Giles was the optimist. "What if we set up a six monthly screening programme, instead of the annual one?" he asked so innocently.

"That would be laughed out of any meeting purely on a cost basis" she replied.

I took the initiative. "I don't want to go on any screening programme. I was on one before and my cancer failed to be picked up. That's just not good enough; I don't want a ticking time bomb inside me."

We all understood what I implied. We left knowing that my case would be put forward at the next medical meeting, and she would contact me in a few days with the outcome.

I sat very comfortably between Bedford and The Lister Hospital and I felt that if I chose to go ahead with surgery, my preference was to do it sooner rather than later. I was aware of the impact of changes to government policies and budgets.

True to her word the specialist called me a few days later and confirmed that it was in my best interest to go ahead with the second mastectomy. I didn't need to wait. I could go ahead as soon as I felt I was ready. With that I knew that I did not have any choice but to go for it. My only concern - I needed Mr Schreuder to perform this operation. And doubts had already been raised.

28

Footprints in the sand

As soon as I put the telephone down from Addenbrooke's, I took a deep long breath as I stared out of my study window. My mum had chopped some branches off a tree in our front garden and asked what I thought of it as I put my head round the front door, to tell her the news. There I was, more concerned about having my boob chopped off. I didn't care about that bloody tree, it only looked beautiful for two weeks of the year, and I really wasn't fussed if it was perfectly shaped or not. I had more important things to worry about. What I quickly realised at that moment was how important it was to change my life for the better, forever. I needed to dedicate my time to getting myself fit and healthy and in great shape to put myself through another lengthy surgical procedure. Contrary to belief, I had really struggled to get over my first operation and the healing process was slow. I didn't want that experience again. I would be in control this time. I put myself on a healthy eating plan the next day and incorporated some exercise into my daily routine. I wasn't capable of anything too strenuous to begin with. A gentle stroll around the block was my limit initially but after a few weeks I managed to increase that to walking around the village after dinner. I felt my energy levels improve as the days slipped by. I was alone with my thoughts, gradually building my strength and within a couple of months I accomplished a four mile circuit. What I didn't realise in the early days of exercising was how I had so easily escaped into an isolated world where I found myself reliving the last few months and coming to terms with how I had escaped death through this life threatening disease. It was emotionally tough; yes I felt great from the benefits of exercise when I had people around me. But when I disappeared off on my own, my mind switched into overdrive and I would walk along crying where no one could see me. Later, I found my thoughts getting deeper and darker as I imagined myself dying and watched my own funeral, listening to the songs that I wanted played. '*Footprints in the Sand*' by Leona Lewis seemed to be my favourite at the time. I imagined Giles and the girls placing white roses on my coffin with tears running down their little cheeks, mouthing how much they loved me. Those same visions appeared daily each time I set off. I even took myself out for a drive and listened to the saddest music that I could find as tears streamed down my cheeks, until one day I felt I couldn't cope anymore and drove to Bedford Hospital. In the Primrose Unit I broke down in front of my chemo nurse. I wasn't coping mentally and nobody else realised. I made a breakthrough that day, particularly when my nurse told me how normal it was to feel this way. Most people experience dark emotions at some point, some as early as diagnosis. After chemo my hormone levels were displaced and it would take time to settle back to normal. I was relieved to discover my anxieties were totally expected and I would rise from these feeling of deep despair. The exercise certainly aided the process and, although not feeling my best, I still ensured that I made time in my day to walk. Gradually I increased to a power walk pace. I started to feel physically improved, and more positive mentally, more inclined to take control. Being on my healthy eating plan combined with the exercise, I was also seeing the results. I kept the exercise momentum going and entered the Hospice ten miles Midnight Walk which was scheduled for three months later. My aim was purely to get myself fit, a personal challenge and importantly an incentive to focus on.

If I didn't have one thing to worry about I quickly found another. Still walking each day I suddenly thought, '...what if Mr Schreuder wasn't prepared to operate on me, what would I do then?' I didn't want the stress or inconvenience of finding someone else; I liked and trusted Mr Schreuder, and I was extremely comfortable at Lister Hospital under his care. I couldn't cope with the thought of going somewhere else and the uncertainty that would entail. I was as calm and relaxed as I possibly could be where I was. That was important to me as it meant that I was less anxious in front of the children and they also knew where I was going, I would be looked after and they were able to see me every day.

29

Surgeon to surf dude, he say 'yes'

The interim period between hospital appointments always seemed to fly by. Shortly before I went back to see Mr Schreuder to discuss the next course of surgery, I started dreaming about him. My mind had really started to play games. The seed had been planted when his registrar had flippantly informed me that Mr Schreuder wasn't able to perform my next operation. I dreamt that he had decided to take a career break from surgery, bleached his hair blonde and became a full time surf dude! Even wearing the white string bracelets and anklets of all surfers.

"Apparently it was something that he needed to get out of his system," his registrar told me, during a consultation, and with that Mr Schreuder entered the room in his surf shorts with his surf board tucked under his arm and shouted "I'm outta here!" and with that he left the hospital building. Finally, I did wake up, thank goodness!

Mr Schreuder was already fully aware and briefed on my decision when I saw him.

"Sarah I've decided because we haven't got your back to use I think the best option for you is the procedure called an, I gap. This will involve removing the inferior gluteus muscle with a little bit of fat from your buttocks and transferring it to the chest," he said, trying to simplify the explanation of complicated surgery.

"Will you be prepared to perform this for me?" I quizzed. I didn't care about anything else. I even knew that he had never carried out this procedure before.

"I'm prepared to do it for you," he confirmed. "But I will have another consultant to assist me, who has carried out this procedure before."

Lucky me, I thought, having two surgeons to myself in theatre.

"....I think it would be a good idea if you met him before the operation as well so he knows what he is dealing with."

I do believe that surgeons are very clever people and surely once he had the tissue that was required, the area he hadn't crossed before - continuing with the rest of the procedure - would surely be the same. I cannot stress how relieved and delighted I was when he agreed to keep me under his wings. I mentioned my dreams to him and he laughed at me. Perhaps he thinks that the life of a surf dude might have been quite an appealing option in hindsight! He was prepared to go ahead with surgery as soon as I was ready for it. I wanted to continue getting myself healthier and more fit and enjoy the summer ahead before I did anything. I really needed to look after myself and put myself in the best possible shape, so we decided to make another appointment for three months to review my progress.

30

My Mission

I have never been more focused on anything in my entire life as I was preparing myself for that operation. I walked between thirty five and forty two miles a week and really felt revitalised for doing so and lost two stone. My hair started to grow back and it was great not having the worry of styling it. It was really dark though - what a shock that was. I had been blonde all my life, very blonde as a child and by the time I reached fifteen I regularly highlighted it, so it was strange seeing myself with dark mousy hair!

I found walking in all weathers exceptionally liberating. It didn't matter when I got extremely soaked in the rain - I was alive and valued everything. I noticed in fine detail the breathtaking scenery around me, the blend in colours of leaves on the trees, the chorus of birds tweeting and the way the cows came to greet me when I walked over the brow of the hill. The little things that I had taken for granted previously. Family walks meant so much more as we headed through the countryside, admiring the beautiful views that surround us: the fields that stretched for miles with the occasional church in the distance. We chatted as we walked. They are such special memories for me now – I will hold them forever. For once, I never complained about my hair getting blown about in the wind. I actually think women look striking when their hair grows back, reflecting their sudden burst of health and vitality. But I couldn't get used to dark hair: I couldn't wait for the highlights. It felt like a real treat visiting the hairdressers' for the first time in nine months - although I will never forget paying eighty nine pounds for the privilege, and no sign of a glass of champagne in sight. I nearly choked when I was presented with the bill; my hair was only an inch long for goodness sake. Needless to say, I found myself a new hairdresser!

Still on the serious mission of exercise I bought myself a little gadget which is probably my best investment - an IPod nano to work in conjunction with the Nike sport. I measured how far I walked, at what speed and exactly how many calories I burnt off. I was obsessed - determined to burn a thousand calories a day. What I failed to burn pounding the streets I ensured I hopped on the treadmill in the garage and burnt off the remainder. I think in many ways my obsessions became a form of proxy control. I controlled what I ate and how much I exercised, whereas I didn't have control on what goes on in my body, when cells decide to go on the rampage.

31

Summer holidays and floods

A whole year had passed now and the school summer holidays were suddenly upon us again and we were ready for our annual jaunt to Jersey and Spain to visit family. I couldn't believe how wonderful I felt. I was impressed with how we, as a family, had conducted ourselves over the last year - from the deep feelings of despair to having my whole life to look forward to. It was really great to have the confidence to wear a bikini and absolutely nobody able to notice the difference. I never imagined that would be possible. I kind of draw the line at going topless or even venturing out onto a nudist beach though! So the registrar who had sat on the end of my hospital bed and told me to be proud of my reconstruction was absolutely right. I am clearly proud of everything that has been done for me, and in many ways wearing a bikini on holiday reflected how I felt within. I felt on top of the world and fantastic when I walked out into the Mediterranean Sea holding hands with Olivia and Annabel.

Shortly after my holiday I met the plastic surgeon who was going to assist Mr Schreuder in theatre. He wanted to meet me to examine me to confirm that I was an ideal candidate for the nature of this kind of surgery. On examination he found a lump on my reconstructed breast. It flawed me. He went on to warn me that this could be a local recurrence. Bearing in mind that I had chosen to be relatively naive, refraining from reading any literature on breast cancer, I had no idea whatsoever that breast cancer could reappear in a breast that fundamentally contained no breast tissue, just fat and muscle from my stomach. Why on earth would I go ahead and have a mastectomy if the risk of reoccurrence could be that quick? I was in complete shock. I had just had the most amazing summer, feeling marvellous, to suddenly relive all of the emotions again so quickly. Naturally I became inconsolable and tearful. I felt so ignorant to this disease that I simply couldn't hurry away in such upset. However I was aware of the consultant's discomfort due to the pressures of a full waiting room outside, and I knew that I was taking too much of his time. But I needed some gesture of empathy and I needed the confirmation from him that we would have a strong bond as we moved forward. I sought that from everyone who treated me.

"I think it is a good idea if I refer you back to Bedford to do a biopsy on this lump, and then come back and see me in six weeks when you know the outcome." I was being eaten up inside - in shock by his words.

"I already have an appointment with Mr Schreuder," I told him, hoping he would tell me to just go along and stick to that appointment.

Instead I was told; "I will go ahead and cancel that appointment for you and you can come back and see me as I am also your consultant now." And he advised the clinic nurse to amend my next appointment.

I immediately felt nauseous. Not only had I just discovered that there was a possibility that the cancer had come back I had lost my backbone - the person that I came to trust so much to operate on me. I didn't have anything against my new consultant apart from him frightening me on our first meeting. But he wasn't the person who had got me through my initial surgery splendidly. As soon as I left the hospital and reached my car I phoned Giles in tears. "He's found a lump and it could be a local recurrence. I didn't know that could happen, and he's cancelled my next appointment, too, with Mr Schreuder. Please can you come home?" I was in a state. Giles was straight on the phone to Mr Schreuder's PA, reinstating my appointment. He, too, was comfortable with my team. I was so grateful to her for organising this for us. She really understood how we felt. We could sense it.

By the end of the week I was back in the out-patients' department at Bedford Hospital, where it had all started, waiting to see my breast consultant. It's such a deserted feeling when you are sitting in that waiting area, going back for what could be your worst nightmare confirmed.

I sat with my stomach in nervous twists, popping to the loo at every opportunity, hoping I didn't miss my turn in my absence. I couldn't help but sit and watch everyone around me. I felt sympathetic to their anxieties as I knew what potentially lay ahead. We were all there for the same reason.

I was called in to see the consultant who went through all the usual formalities. You can't really say it was good to see them again because that is just not true in the nicest sense of the word. He examined me and then advised that it was necessary to have a biopsy, which he didn't like doing to me. Then he sent me off for another ultra sound to double check everything; they needed to be cautious. He felt that it may be some fatty tissue, fat necrosis they call it, but he couldn't be certain. He didn't appear too overly concerned, though, which was quite reassuring. The ultra sound came back as slightly inconclusive, mainly due to me not having any breast tissue with any glands - just fat and muscle. Again my consultant was quite positive - you can always tell by their reactions and facial expressions - that I didn't really have anything to worry about but told me to come back a week later for the final results. Thankfully those results came back as benign.

In preparation for the second mastectomy my breast surgeon requested I had a mammogram on my natural breast. This ensured that it was absolutely clear of disease. If there were any areas for concern then I would have an MRI scan, so that they knew what to expect when it came to surgery. Luckily I didn't need to have an MRI scan as the report came back clear. One thing I was certain of was that I could not live with a ticking time bomb inside me. I had just experienced the feeling of sudden fear that cancer had returned and that was sufficient to confirm that I could not live this way for the rest of my life.

My reinstated appointment with Mr Schreuder finally came and I apologised profusely in the first instance for causing such a fuss. He knew at that point he wasn't going to get rid of me that easily and transfer me to another surgeon! I knew that he completely understood my motives for wanting to stay as his patient. I was eager to get moving with the operation and we pencilled a date for roughly seven weeks.

Great I thought. I'm well and truly into my home stretch and the end of the road.

32

Health and fitness

I have never been as obsessed about anything in my life as I was in those final seven weeks. I was so focused on ensuring that I was as fit and healthy as I could possibly be. I was not going to put myself on that operating table in anything but perfect condition, and that had to come from the inside out.

Every opportunity I had to exercise, I made sure I did. It became my ritual and I felt magnificent for doing it. After dinner when the family sat down to watch Eastenders, I took myself into the garage and ran on the treadmill for half an hour, beads of sweat pouring from me. I loved it, it was infectious, and I wanted to do more and more. I drank gallons of water a day, believing that it would simply plump out my blood vessels to prepare them for surgery- a rumour I'd heard. I drank close to three litres a day and I eliminated coffee and alcohol. I replaced my wine with soda and lime if we went out anywhere, and I didn't notice that I missed it. I maintained a healthy diet. Breakfast generally consisted of yoghurt and chopped apple, with a few teaspoons of pumpkin and sunflower seeds to bulk it out. I always had a tuna salad for lunch with lots of peppers - they are a great antioxidant - and an apple for pudding. My evening meal varied between chicken or fish with roasted vegetables or salad. I stuck to this religiously, well apart from a Friday night when I may have had a few crisps and dips with some sparkling water, just so I could join Giles in a spot of indulgence!

As the date for surgery drew near I boosted my intake of fresh fruit and vegetables with the introduction of my creative juicing recipes. I juiced spinach, broccoli, carrots, peppers, oranges, apples, strawberries all together. It was thick and green. It looked disgusting but actually didn't taste half as bad as it looked, especially when served in a tall glass with plenty of ice cubes. In fact the ice cubes are a must! I definitely preferred mixing everything together rather than making purely a vegetable or fruit juice. The fruit sweetened the vegetable taste, particularly the spinach. My skin looked completely unblemished, and I felt splendid. I even added a bit of interval training into my daily exercise regime and by the time my operation date came I knew that I had done everything in my power to get myself as fit as I could and ready for this operation. I seriously could not have done more to help myself.

33

Ticking clock

So there I was again, with my devoted husband, who had watched me go through so much, unable to take away some of my worries, in the admittance ward at Lister Hospital waiting for all the surgeons to arrive. How lucky was I having three consultants operate on me that day? Sorry to those who may have had their operations cancelled or had to wait longer than anticipated in clinic, due to insufficient staffing, but they had me to take care of! Phew! My breast surgeon came from Bedford and I had my two plastic surgeons who would work together, sharing their skills and expertise. They were joined on that occasion by a very eager, enthusiastic and chirpy registrar who was the first to bound into the consulting room and introduce himself as Amir, grinning like a Cheshire cat, probably loving the challenge that waited. To be part of the team who would perform the first I-gap operation at the hospital. Even understanding that, I felt confident.

I felt much less anxious about the anaesthetic and going into theatre than I had done the previous year; mainly because it was my choice. I wanted to eliminate all risk, and it was only me that put myself in this position. All marked up and ready to go in my hospital gown and my dressing gown, I casually asked the surgeons: "So what are you going to listen to in theatre today then?"

They always played music in the medical drama Holby City.

"What would you like us to play for you Sarah?" Mr Schreuder asked. I thought anything by *Take That* but I don't think they featured on his playlist. If I had been quick enough I could have replied with, "I don't mind but just 'wake me up before you go go' will do," but as always, I'm too slow! With that they left me to get themselves ready for theatre. It only felt like a few minutes before I was called. Giles and I, along with a nurse, who carried all my belongings, made our way to the theatre area. I felt calm and that time just kissed Giles goodbye at the doors leading into the theatre area. It wasn't until I sat on my hospital bed and the anaesthetist came to see me - the same one that put me to sleep the previous year - with a huge grin on his face, just the same as before, that I burst into tears again and actually realised what was about to happen and just how awful I would feel the following morning. As I lay waiting to be knocked out in the anaesthetic room, I reminded myself not to touch the pain relief trigger when I came round, even if I desperately needed it, because I knew it made me feel so nauseous and delirious. In no time I was out for the count, again.

Coming around in the recovery room after the operation was consequently so different. It really felt like a totally different experience. As soon as I was stabilised I was completely alert and didn't feel I had been through anything. I even joked with the staff and asked if they had remembered to operate. I felt so proud of myself. I truthfully believe that the fitness work I had done had really paid off, a complete contrast to how I felt to the last operation. When the nurse came from the ward to collect me, I recognised her voice and remembered her name instantly. She had been the same nurse that I had broken down in front of last year. She was delighted that I had remembered her name and I chatted to her as we went back to ward. I was wide awake and felt no pain at all. I felt fantastic just for taking great care of myself.

When I arrived on the ward I was put into a room on my own and was monitored every half an hour by the nurses, this time wide awake and not minding the disturbance. I couldn't wait until I saw Giles in the morning. I knew he would be so pleased to see me feeling and looking so great and alert. But within a couple of hours of going back to the ward two new registrars came into my room to examine me and told me that they may have to take me back to theatre and to prepare myself. The nurse had noticed the flap, the new skin that they used to cover the breast, had started to change colour and was turning a darker shade, which suggested that the new tissue may not have got a sufficient blood supply to it, and she was concerned. I was closely monitored and they promised to come back and see me later.

I felt anxious again. This time not about the prospect of going back to theatre but because I noticed how incredibly young these registrars looked and I didn't know if they would have the experience to take me back to theatre, especially on their own. I think that is a sign of getting a bit older. They came back to see me later on, but, thank goodness, they didn't need to get me back to theatre. The appearance of the flap was unchanged. Contrary to what may have been taking place I still felt fabulous in myself and under no circumstance did I want to press the pain relief trigger.

Just before eight the following morning Amir burst into my room and I greeted him with a huge smile that spoke volumes. "I can't believe how great I feel, I'd prepared myself for feeling terrible, like I had been run over by a bus. Are you sure you actually operated on me yesterday?" I laughed, surprised at how I recovered. I felt seriously great.

"Amir, the registrars on the night shift came to see me and told me they might need to take me back to theatre, they thought the flap looked dark."

"No. You won't need to go back to theatre, the operation went as brilliantly as it could, although it did take us a little longer than anticipated," he reassured.

When Mr Schreuder came to see me I was still beaming. I looked at him, completely touched that he had done everything that I had asked of him. No wonder he had allowed me to trust him to the extent that I had. I couldn't stop smiling and thanking him as he examined me. Quietly, though, he obviously had his concerns when he mentioned that I wasn't out of the woods yet - a phrase that I had not heard him say before.

If anything was going to happen - like the flap failing for example - it would happen within the first seventy two hours of surgery.

Giles also came to see early in the morning. He hadn't managed to see me the previous evening as I was delayed in theatre, and didn't actually arrive on the ward until much later in the evening. He was speechless when he saw me sitting up and smiling. He immediately got his mobile phone and took a photograph of me and distributed it to my friends and family, thankfully not on facebook though! "You look brilliant. I wasn't expecting you to be awake and lucid." He assumed that I would be drowsy from the previous day's heavy dose of anaesthetic. I even made him go down to the hospital shop and stock up on magazines for me – I needed something to help me pass the time away.

As I lay in bed flicking through a magazine, I began to feel really cold, and even called the nursing staff to get me another blanket to put over me. My room wasn't as warm as it had been after my first reconstruction. I understood that following the flap surgery you needed to sustain a tropical room temperature for at least seventy two hours. But nobody actually questioned my room temperature when they came to see me and I trusted them. I was still closely monitored and examined every hour and all appeared to be fine. I spent the day on a high as I felt so relieved to have eliminated the potential risk of cancer returning to my other breast. That ticking time bomb had gone forever and it was all over. I knew that Giles wanted to bring the girls to see me that evening and I was so happy and proud that they could see me bright and cheerful and understand that I was well. Annabel came straight to me and kissed me and sat beside my bed holding my hand, curious to know what all the tubes were and what they were draining away.

"How are you feeling mummy?" Confirmation that she was so grown up for her years. She was only six, and had probably needed to grow up prematurely due to our situation. She portrayed a really caring side to her otherwise quirky demeanour, intrigued to know what all the other gadgets were used for in my room. Once Olivia had gently kissed me, she took her place at the end of the bed and found reading all the celebrity gossip in my well stocked magazine pile far more captivating. A trait very similar to my own, our inbuilt coping mechanism - shut out what we can't cope with and pretend it's not real.

I was exhausted by early evening and desperate for a good night's sleep. But that wasn't going to be an option due to the regular observations and examinations being taken throughout the night. The nurse came into my very dimly lit room, shone a small torch in my face as she poked and prodded my chest, then mouthed "it's fine" before walking out again. It felt as though no sooner had I drifted off to sleep I was disturbed again to go through the same routine. Consequently it was a really long night before morning arrived with the sound of the rattling early morning tea trolley. I was quite uncomfortable lying in bed all day and night, in exactly the same position. I couldn't move very much and make myself more comfortable due to the little twinges of pain but I was stubborn and refused to press the morphine pump.

It was Friday morning, the big ward round morning. Mr Schreuder came to see with at least six medical staff with him. As he examined me I don't recall him saying anything. It was quite unusual for him to be quiet. I sensed that he was concerned. He looked at the reconstruction and frowned as he asked a nurse to pass him a pin with which he proceeded to prick the flap area. Thankfully I no longer had any feeling in the breast area. I assumed that was to check the colour of the blood, maybe if it's a bright red it's healthy if it's darker it's more likely to be unhealthy and the tissue in the process of dying. He still didn't say anything to me, I looked at Amir, who held my hand and mouthed it was fine to me. I knew Mr Schreuder and I knew by the look on his face and his body language that he wasn't happy. He didn't need to say anything to me. I suppose what baffled him was the flap looked visibly darker than perhaps it should have done, but when pricked the blood was bright red. Like my first breast reconstruction, I still wasn't confident, or ready to have a look at my new breast for myself. Instead I observed the reactions of everyone around me.

When the nurses came in to see me they thought that it would be a good idea if I tried to get myself out of bed and into the chair. I admit, I did press the pain relief to get myself up and out of bed, I wasn't that brave! It was really bizarre sitting up; I didn't feel any different to how I felt normally having my natural boob. For a few days after my first reconstruction it really felt like I had a heavy concrete slab across my chest, but this time I didn't feel a thing. I just felt normal. I managed to wash and freshen up and put on a nice newly ironed pair of pyjamas that had a strong smell of Comfort fabric conditioner - so comfy and reminiscent of home, to put on along with new slippers, especially after spending a couple of days in the NHS gown.

Mr Schreuder returned with another consultant who I had never met before, for a second opinion on the appearance of the flap. I knew he wasn't happy but as I sat in the chair beside the window with the daylight illuminating the room, it gave a different colour and tone to the flap and it looked much healthier.

"I feel much happier now," Mr Schreuder confirmed.

On the Saturday morning I woke early and managed to walk to the toilet unaided. Whilst there, I decided it was time to be strong and take a look at my new breast.

As I pulled my pyjama top to the side and looked down, I felt sick with shock. There was a massive dip in the middle of it and the flap really looked really dark to me, much darker than the tone of bruising and a completely different size. I started to cry. I had made the decision to have the second mastectomy to eliminate all risks of the cancer coming back, but I had taken away a perfectly healthy breast to be replaced by something that horrified me, and it was only me who had put me in that position. Worried and distraught I returned to my room and closed the door. I didn't want to see anyone. I just needed time to be on my own to think - almost mourn - what I had lost. I knew I had friends coming in to see me later in the afternoon and I didn't feel up to seeing anyone. I didn't want to feel pressured to sit there and make small talk. I wanted time to withdraw from everyone. I was so disappointed. I phoned Giles in tears, a state that he was accustomed to from time to time. I told him I didn't want to see anyone, to call my friends and cancel their visit. I knew in myself that my reconstruction didn't look right. It certainly didn't look anything like the first one – sufficient to base my judgement. I couldn't even stomach a cup of tea when the trolley came round at breakfast. I felt so sick and abandoned.

Amir came to examine me before he started his theatre list. He could tell that I wasn't myself. I was distant and vague, preoccupied with my thoughts and didn't really have much to say. The flap didn't appear to change colour so it wasn't deteriorating in appearance. He promised that he would come back and see me at the end of the day when his theatre list was completed. It was at that point that I became aware of the big clock that was strategically placed right in the centre of the opposite wall from my bed, so I had been looking straight at it. All I did was watch the time tick by and check the flap every now and again. I checked myself to see if the flap changed colour and hoped that it suddenly developed a slight pink tone, but whenever I looked it appeared unchanged and my heart sank yet again. I felt sick, couldn't eat, not even a square of Galaxy chocolate, and couldn't even attempt to read as I lost all levels of concentration. My only point of focus became that clock on the opposite wall, where the hands ticked by almost in slow motion.

When Amir returned that evening I broke down. I couldn't shield my emotions anymore. I didn't want to be left in the physical state I was currently in and I wasn't aware of my options.

"There is so much that we can do for you. We'll be able to make it absolutely perfect. Stop worrying - it will all be fine, we are not going to leave you until you are completely satisfied with the result." Such positive words. I appreciated his enthusiasm, the bounds of energy that he had. He genuinely wanted a positive outcome for me and was so personable in the manner in which he spoke, but he could have spoken to me with all his enthusiasm until he was blue in the face. I had not sensed the same positive vibes from Mr Schreuder the previous day and he was where my trust and confidence lay. Until he told me that he would ensure that I would be really happy with the result and there were lots of options available to me to make it perfect I would not be satisfied. I had read articles that state how important it is to trust your consultant and to make sure that you 'choose' the right one. I hadn't needed to choose mine. I was allocated him through the system, a system that understood and valued his expertise and, if you ever find yourself in a situation similar to mine, you will understand that that is worth the weight in gold to you. That's what I felt I had.

When Giles came to see me that evening I was low. I knew that things were not going as planned for me. I wanted to show him what I meant. Strangely he didn't want to have a look, and yet he had been so keen the first time around. He didn't even try and reassure me that it would all be fine and lift my spirits. Maybe he had just sensed it all from me. Deep down, if I'm honest, I don't think he really knew how to handle the situation. We hadn't planned for anything going wrong and he couldn't offer me the words or actions that I needed. I asked him to go home to the girls, and he did as instructed.

Sunday came and went. All I did was check the flap but there was no change. My instinct told me not to raise my hopes of a sudden healing. Against this notion, while I knew that the flap didn't look healthy, until I was told otherwise, I really had to remain as positive and focused as

I could. By Monday morning I felt groggy. Light headed, dizzy and I had a thumping headache. I suppose the anxiety had started to take its toll. I felt miserable all day.

When I woke the following morning I felt much brighter and thought that I was well enough to be discharged and looked forward to going home. I got up early to get dressed, put a little make-up on so I felt more human and presentable and went for little walk along the hospital corridor to help build some strength. I bumped into Amir.

"I can't believe I feel so much better today, and I'm looking forward to going home," I told him.

"Good." He answered brightly but non-committed. "I'm pleased for you," he said, as I made my way back to my room.

Mr Schreuder came to see me shortly after eight, accompanied by Amir and the ward sister, and examined me. Then sat on the bed, held my hand and said "Sarah, I'm so sorry."

"Has it failed?" I guessed.

"Yes" he replied. I immediately thought it was something that I may have done. "What did I do wrong?" I asked trying to seek an explanation.

"You've done absolutely nothing wrong. It's not your fault."

I had done everything in my power to ensure that I was as healthy as possible for the procedure. I couldn't cry. In some ways I wasn't surprised that I was hearing this news. I was half expecting it subconsciously. What I don't understand is why I got myself up and dressed that morning - denial perhaps, or hope. I always knew that the operation had a ninety five percent success rate, but the thought that it may potentially fail never entered my mind at any time. I certainly didn't blame the people around me.

"Please don't worry Sarah, there are still plenty of options available to you and we are all a team. I promise that I will see you through to the other side and we will get through it together," he reassured. "But, in the meantime, I need to take you back to theatre to remove all of the donor tissue and to fit an expander implant, which will allow the saved skin to stretch for when we are ready to have another attempt." He added: "We've still got another I-gap procedure as you have the other cheek to use."

I knew all of the medical team were as disappointed as me to see the operation fail. They are a team of perfection-ists at the end of the day and they wanted a successful result, as much as I did.

I was taken back to theatre the following day, not sur-prisingly feeling very anxious of yet another anaesthetic. You would think that after a few operations my fears would start to fade, but I think mine seemed to grow even greater. Psychologically, I think it was an inbuilt coping mechanism that I had, in the sense that if I focused so much on the anaesthetic it didn't leave any space for thoughts of what was happening beyond the anaesthetic - which in actual fact, frightened me more! The anaesthetist – new to me - couldn't find any veins in my arm or hand. After numerous attempts she resorted to using a vein in my foot. I felt the cold fluid travel all the way up my leg and then I felt a sudden dull ache right in the base of my spine. I panicked for a split second, and then I was fast asleep.

Waking up in recovery, I recall thinking that the implant didn't feel any different, nothing like I thought it would. When I was taken back on the ward the nursing staff were all excited for me, but they were going to leave Mr Schreuder to explain. Confused I waited for him to finish his operating list so he could come and see me. I couldn't wait for him to explain. As soon as he had finished in theatre he came upstairs to tell me the news. "When we opened you up and took a look at all the tissue it looked really healthy and had a good blood supply going to it, I just couldn't take it away. I need to give it another chance and only time will tell. We're not out of woods yet but fingers crossed" He seemed happy for me – and the team. "I even arranged for the hospital photographer to take images as I was surprised that the tissue still appeared healthy." He added: "For now, we just needed to play a waiting game."

I telephoned Giles and told him the great news and how excited everyone was. I asked him to bring in a couple of tins of chocolates for the nursing staff and one for Mr Schreuder and his team, get *Heroes* because in my mind they were my unsung heroes. I thought that would be quite a straight forward task to ask as it was late November and all the shops stocked tins of Heroes for Christmas. Giles went to six supermarkets on his way from Milton Keynes to Stevenage, and each one had sold out of them. So he decided to use his initiative and turned up at hospital with a tin of *Roses* and a tin of *Quality Street* only to be met by a rather underwhelming reaction. I couldn't believe that he had chosen those chocolates. Couldn't he comprehend that the name on the tin was meant to say it all? I told him he hadn't tried hard enough and he wasn't that impressed with me and looking back I really don't blame him. Particularly as the hospital shop downstairs sold them. I could have got them myself and saved him the inconvenience after work when all he wanted to do was to come and see me. Of course I never mentioned that to him.

I was sent home in time for the weekend with the instruction to return to the clinic on Monday morning to see Amir to confirm that everything was healing properly. Apart from feeling very tired and jaded and looking very pale, I was fine in myself. I wasn't in any pain at all and we just had a very quiet weekend in front of a roaring fire and the TV watching films together, regrouping and catching up, with the occasional friend popping in for a cup of tea and offering to help me with anything that needed doing.

Monday morning soon came round and we could have put our car on autopilot to take us to Lister with the number of times that Giles had driven over there. When I was examined by Amir he wasn't happy with the condition of the flap and recommended that I returned the following day to see Mr Schreuder and to bring my overnight bag as I may be readmitted.

So there I was yet again, Ward 11b with Kathy, my chauffeur and company for the day and my solid friend of twenty years. We saw Mr Schreuder and Amir together and it was agreed that it would be best if they went ahead and removed every ounce of tissue and replaced it with the implant.

"We can put you on this afternoon's theatre list or you can wait until tomorrow and go on Mr Schreuder's list?" Amir explained.

"Oh I've had breakfast this morning," feeling that I couldn't possibly go into theatre after eating - but actually too frightened to be operated on by anybody else. They knew what I was like and put me on the list for the following day and I was readmitted.

"Amir I'm really nervous about the anaesthetic," I confessed. "Last week I had a really unpleasant experience of being put to sleep."

I tried to explain my experience. He got straight on the case and arranged for a consultant anaesthetist to be available for me the following day.

This may sound institutionalised but I had a really charming day with Kathy in the hospital whilst waiting for my bed to become available. We ventured downstairs and had lunch in the restaurant, tuna sandwich and a packet of crisps and then treated ourselves to a massive bag of pick and mix sweets from the shop and bought all the latest magazines, trying hard not to duplicate any from the previous week that I may have already read. We then positioned ourselves in the day room and read, ate and talked all day laughing at celeb stories in the magazines. Katie Price and Peter Andre seemed to feature highly - Peter unhappy with the amount of cosmetic surgery Katie was obsessed with having. He was apparently worried about the amount of anaesthetic and how it would be ageing for her. I did question that with Mr Schreuder and he did make me laugh when he replied, "Well let's put it this way, it's not going to make you look any younger."

It may sound a slight contradiction in terms for a very anxious patient to feel really relaxed within the hospital. I don't like the surgery side of things but the actual department was really friendly and I was treated exceptionally well. If you are not familiar with a hospital's surroundings, it can be quite daunting but I actually felt at home and comfortable there. I appreciated the quality of care and the amiable manner in which it was delivered - it was ultimately of utmost importance to me.

Waiting to go to theatre the following day was dreadful. I wasn't due to go to theatre until later in the afternoon and I just spent the entire day with a really splitting headache. I was nervous of the anaesthetic and I just told the nurse that I really couldn't do it and I wouldn't be going to theatre. Unfortunately, on that occasion I didn't actually have any choice in the matter as I was prone to infection. She was able to give me paracetamol to try to relieve my headache and I just lay on my bed feeling drained and exhausted. Eventually I was called and wheeled down to theatre. When I was taken into the anaesthetic room I ended up with exactly the same anaesthetist as last week and I panicked and sobbed. I don't know where I got the energy from to cry. Just as the anaesthetist was about to stick the needle in my hand Amir came through the doors and held my hand as I was put to sleep. These simple gestures are unheard of within the NHS and I was so touched with that level of care.

I can't recall being in recovery or being wheeled back up to the ward after the operation. I didn't feel at all right in myself and when Giles came to see me in the evening I could barely open my eyes to talk to him. The look on his face when I did have the energy to open my eyes shocked me. His eyes were red and watery as if he had been crying for some time. He looked at me and said that I didn't deserve all of this misfortune. My complexion was really grey and I looked ill and he felt that life was just so unfair. It is the only time that he has ever felt or said anything of this nature through our whole journey. His eyes were filled with tears but I just wanted him to go home. I was too tired to talk. He held my hand for a few minutes and gave me a kiss and then left me to sleep. During the night I was breathing but I wasn't getting any oxygen and every now and then my head would throb. I started to panic and pressed for the nurse to come and help me. I really wasn't feeling very well and I knew that something wasn't right. I don't normally like to disturb nurses and this was the only time that I ever did, but I was scared. The nurse came and took my observations and then called for the night doctor. When the doctor arrived she immediately took a blood test from my groin and requested a scan as soon as possible to double check that I didn't have a blood clot. Thankfully, the scan revealed that I didn't have a blood clot - instead one of my lungs had collapsed. I was prescribed good old fashioned bed rest. After a couple of days I started feeling better. However, if I stood up for any prolonged length of time, I felt incredibly faint and light headed so I wasn't able to do anything strenuous.

I really appreciated my time in hospital and it most definitely gave me the rest that I desperately needed. When I get home I can't help but start to get involved in daily chores again, thinking I can do so much more than I am actually up to. On that occasion when I got home I had to listen to my body for a change. I was literally physically unable to do anything. Three operations in three weeks had certainly taken their toll on my body and it was crying out for some rest. I couldn't even prise myself up off the sofa to attend the girls' Christmas performances at school which I'd promised them that I would be well enough to make. Unfortunately, I was exhausted and could not draw an ounce of strength from my body to get myself there. But at least they had me at home to share in their excitement when they returned.

34

The booby prize and Christmas

A breast after a reconstruction still feels quite soft, fleshy and natural, but the expander implant that I had, felt very different and unnatural. It was very firm; I found it impossible to lie on my stomach. Every time I leant against anything on that side the port used for saline solution injections - that sits just below the surface of the skin - would catch on everything, causing a sharp excruciating pain and bruising. I still don't understand how anyone can go ahead and have enormous, unnatural implants, although I appreciate that it is obviously a totally different scenario if you actually choose to have this procedure. For me as far as I was concerned, I had what I can only describe as the booby prize. The quicker I could get rid of it the better I would feel again.

Christmas was approaching, with only a couple of weeks to go. Thank goodness for the invention of internet shopping. I don't know what I would have done without it that year, managing to do all my presents and food buying on line. We had planned to have a really quiet

Christmas with just the four of us. As always I had gone over the top with food – so I invited my friend Deborah and her children for Christmas day, on the proviso that she cooked Christmas dinner. I felt numb over Christmas. I was disappointed to have worked so hard on getting myself in shape for the final stretch of my treatment and yet at the final hurdle it had all gone against me. Giles was sensitive to my feeling of despair and always did his best to raise my spirits during this distressed time.

My healing post surgery was absolutely incredible considering my chest had been opened and closed on three occasions. I had healed externally in two weeks and my scaring was so neat. It took me a month to feel rejuvenated again and begin to think about getting back to my fitness regime. Over the course of time I have realised what a colossal, positive impact exercise has and the benefits that is has played both physically and mentally in my well being and how it now plays a vital role in my life. However, I decided to take a break until after Christmas when I vowed to start again on New Year's Day which would have given me a whole six week break from the date of my second mastectomy.

I still felt quite uncomfortable with the implant. Maybe that was influenced by my awareness that it was only ever going to be a temporary measure, so psychologically I naturally made the verdict that it was appalling and I did not need to become familiar to it and would therefore never become accepting of it. It felt unpleasant and I disliked it. I tried to describe to Giles how it felt so he could understand, but his world and the world of implants would never collide - how could he ever understand? Anyway the implant was never a long term option for me due to the dosage of radiotherapy I had received, and I was also susceptible to lots of infections which could eventually result in more surgery to either remove or replace it. So I had no alternative in my mind. The best option for me was to consider another reconstruction. Giles and I discussed this at great length. We were both so touched with the wonderful care that I had received at The Lister Hospital under the overall guidance of my consultant - Giles always refers to him as Fred (it's a man thing) but he's always Mr Schreuder to me - that we both felt very solidly that we would like to continue under his care and proficiency.

We both attended my out-patient appointment just after Christmas, when it was our intention to discuss the options available to me for surgery and to inflate the implant. I didn't want to have another I gap procedure as it had failed me. I recall Mr Schreuder explaining a new procedure that is performed using the muscle and tissue from the inner thigh, which could be performed at a hospital in London and he was more than happy to refer me to another plastic surgeon. Alternatively I could stay where I was, as I still had another buttock to use, and he was more than happy to perform this for me. Giles and I looked at each other and decided instantly that the second option was our preferred choice. It was unquestionable, we both knew Mr Schreuder; we believed that he would not put himself in a situation that was beyond his capabilities. He knew what condition my blood vessels were in and what difficulties he may incur. He also knew how much it meant to me, and most importantly, he had seen me work so hard to get myself as fit as I possibly could to help myself. He understood how focused I was. I wanted to be where people cared. I thought, due to the procedure carrying a ninety five percent success rate, if the operation did go wrong, I knew that the team would do their absolute best for me. I could never be given a hundred percent guarantee that it would be successful wherever I went, so as far as I was concerned I was in the best place with the best surgeon, and that is what I needed. We put a date in the diary for April, when it would be the school Easter Holidays, and I could send the girls away to Spain for a holiday with my mum and dad and go ahead with the second I-gap attempt.

35

So many unanswered questions

As soon as January arrived, Giles and I went out walking in our Christmas woolly hats and completed an eight mile circuit. Not bad for the first time out post surgery and I was amazed as I walked with ease. It was biting cold, but all wrapped up, I felt really vigorous and appreciated the return to the great outdoors exposed to the frosty air. I loved that ritual. After a few days of getting into the swing of walking I rather hastily attempted to run but failed miserably. I felt nauseous with the discomfort from the indescribable sensation from the impact of the wobbling motion of my newly shaped lower bottom. I felt bizarre and had no choice but to continue with walking. From that day on I was back on my mission - to work towards the date planned for surgery and to be in the best possible physical shape. I even went as far as developing obsessive compulsive disorder. I felt that I had failed if I had not organised my day to allow sufficient time to exercise. I needed to burn a thousand calories each day and if I could do more, I did.

I saw Mr Schreuder every fortnight as he inflated the implant. It was during that period that all my reasons for remaining under his care were reinforced to me. I have always been incredibly anxious and he read me like a book - able to assess my concerns and reassure me. I knew that he wouldn't put himself in a position to be responsible in attempting another I gap procedure, knowing that it was my final option if he really felt that he wasn't capable. He managed to alleviate my concerns through every consultation that I had and I felt uplifted (there's a pun) in the knowledge that I was clearly in the best hands. He was also aware of my ever increasing issue regarding the anaesthetic which heightened my anxiety, particularly at night time. Inevitably, it was the start of a new routine as I regularly got out of bed, made myself a cup of coffee and logged onto my work computer in the middle of the night. This was how I managed to sustain the level of exercise I carried out. I needed extra hours in the day. Mr Schreuder arranged an appointment with the anaesthetist who would be in charge on the day to talk through all of my apprehensions – or sheer terror. The anaesthetist couldn't understand my fears, I'd recovered from hours of anaesthetic already, and my body could cope. He concluded he would put me to sleep using gas to ease my concerns.

It was three months after my second mastectomy that my breast care nurse telephoned me to establish how I was recovering following surgery and was concerned about how I was coping mentally particularly following the unsuccessful reconstructive procedure. She had always been aware that I had a great support network around me with all my friends and family and I also understood that I was able to contact her at anytime if I felt I needed that extra support. But I believe the main purpose for that call was to discuss the lab results from the mastectomy which they now had. The breast surgeon had requested she try to bring my pending out-patient appointment forward in order for him to discuss those results with me. Now I know that appointments are changed for many reasons but generally when they are changed they are made for a later date not an earlier one. I was instantly concerned. She knew that I would sit and worry and did her best to reassure me that all was fine, but to no avail. She sensed by the tone of my voice that I was not able to wait until the end of the following week, the next available appointment, to find out. She didn't want me to worry. She told me the results over the phone. Analysis had shown a DCIS, (Ductal Carcinoma in Situ). This was a non invasive cancerous growth found within the duct of the breast. It was classified as non invasive because the growth hadn't spread beyond the duct into any surrounding breast tissue. DCIS can also be referred to as pre cancerous cells which never revert to healthy cells so there is always the risk that they can become invasive over a period of time.

I felt instantly emotional, completely shocked. I assumed that everything had been healthy; after all I hadn't heard anything for three months believing that no news was good news. Bang goes that theory. Most importantly I felt thankful that I had acted on my instinct in the removal. There must have been an angel looking down on me helping me reach that decision. In contrast to the relief that I felt, for a few moments I also felt a huge amount of terror: why was it there? Surely chemotherapy would have prevented any growth developing. Why didn't it destroy those cells? Why was it not picked up in screening from the mammogram taken six weeks before my surgery? Why were comparisons not made with the previous years' mammogram?

Now Giles understands why a screening programme was not an option for me. All thoughts entered my mind. There I was, right before the eyes of an entire medical team, and it was there inside me - a disease that nobody could see. Yet I felt the best that I had felt for a long time. I was positively glowing with healthiness. Thank goodness I made that choice to go ahead and have the mastectomy. If I hadn't taken that decision without delay I would have no choice now - and the consequences of lost time don't bear thinking about.

I still have many unanswered questions but at the end of the day I realise that I have done everything possible that I can. I always maintain I have had the best medical and surgical treatment available to me. On reflection, I think my breast surgeon was as surprised as I was. Just like the rest of the team he wanted to do his very best for me and really didn't expect the DCIS result. I had to move on and enjoy the rest of my life, learn to stop worrying, even though I still wanted to have a new attempt at the reconstruction.

36

What a day of relaxation

I have always found it difficult to build strong friendships with cancer patients, even the first time. I actually sought comfort in one though – Bev, also successfully treated for breast cancer. We were at the same stage of treatment when we met, introduced through a mutual friend, although we were being treated at different hospitals. Bev became my bosom buddy and we shared lots in common in terms of the psychological challenges we faced. We were both due to have our reconstructive surgery at around the same time. To help prepare and de-stress before our surgery dates we treated ourselves to a 'Relaxation Day' at Champneys in Henlow. On arrival we excitably booked ourselves into the relaxation class which we felt was essential for us. Just before the class started we grabbed pillows and blankets and settled onto our mats as we listened to the tranquil music playing quietly in the background. Then the instructor's voice took hold of me. As we lay there she told us to relax, let your body fall to the floor, release your body to the ground, let every bit fall, bit by bit, firstly your head, then your shoulders, your arms, your fingers right through to your finger tips, release them to the ground. I heard someone snoring; he was so relaxed he had fallen asleep. I cried, the voice I heard was the anaesthetist who had struggled to get me to sleep, with the image of her with a syringe in her hand looking up at it, tapping it in preparation to inject to put me out of my misery. My mind was completely irrational; I couldn't get the anaesthetists' silhouette out of my mind. I came out of the class feeling anything other than relaxed. I was emotionally drained. Anxiety and stress plays mayhem with your mind and after that experience I even ended up cancelling my next hospital appointment. I just needed some time out from hospital and the environment. I must have been in a bad way! Poor old Bev, she had treated me to that day, and it had reduced me to a wreck. It's actually quite funny because our recollections of that day are so different from each others. Bev remembers how relaxed we both were, as we sat in the conservatory oblivious to the snow falling outside, chatting away, drinking cups of tea, comparing our fearful and uneasy anticipations of surgery, making light of the bum lift and the tummy tucks to shield ourselves. We left it as late as possible to make our way home. It was only when we got outside we realised how much snow had fallen, how foggy it was and I dreaded driving home in it. Typically, Bev lives in the only village in Bedfordshire with hills in it and I hated driving home alone after I dropped her off. As I reached the top of her road my car skidded towards the T-junction - I decided to make an SOS call to Giles to rescue me, abandoning my car on the side of road.

37

Let's plump up those blood vessels

Health farm relaxations classes aside, my state of mind must be powerful, able to block out my life's misfortunes. Through the astonishment of discovering that I had a lucky escape with the DCIS, and still feeling frightened over the surgery I still had it within me to remain focused. I continued exercising, avoided alcohol and ate healthily and supported this with lots of juicing again. I felt I needed to increase my level of activity so added running on the treadmill every night in the garage, honestly believing that all the exercise would be plumping out the blood vessels. I never did discover if that was really the case. My operation date was set for the 15th April and Olivia and Annabel would be going to Spain to stay with my mum and dad whilst I was in hospital, as it was the Easter holidays. The girls were very excited about having a holiday to look forward to – a distraction for them though I'm told they said a prayer for mummy every night.

As the girls flew out to the Mediterranean sunshine to enjoy a couple of weeks being spoilt by nanny and granddad, I had a couple of days to myself in anticipation of my operation. I don't want to sound boring and repetitive but I spent those consuming pints of juice, drinking plenty of water and exercising. I even got up at half past four on the morning of my operation and did a five kilometre run on the treadmill before I got myself showered and ready for hospital where I was admitted at 7am.

I actually felt surprisingly calm on arrival. I understood what would happen, having been through it before and I had felt fine immediately following surgery. What had slowed my recovery was the need to go back to theatre, and that wasn't going to be necessary this time around, so it didn't faze me. Above all I trusted my surgeon. I knew Mr Schreuder did all of his homework and research allowing him to be confident in what he was about to do. He knew I trusted him completely. I felt so relaxed. I even told Giles not to walk me down to the theatre area as I was absolutely fine and we said our goodbyes. I knew that this time I would be put to sleep with gas. Therefore, I didn't worry about needles. The anaesthetist would address that once I was fast asleep.

38

Gasping

I will remember coming round from that operation forever.

The words – an understatement. "Sarah, it's Thursday morning, we've been in theatre for 25 hours and we are taking you to HDU so we can keep a close eye on you. We took a little bit longer than we thought."

I felt like I was being pushed through a tunnel of plastic. The next time I opened my eyes I was in the high dependency unit and Giles was there to see me. He told me not to talk and just held my hand and told me how much he loved me. I declared that if the operation didn't work that time around I was never going to put myself in this situation again.

He hardly recognised me as I had been pumped with so much fluid in theatre I was so swollen. He thought I looked like Heather, a character in the popular TV soap Eastenders. I, on the other hand thought he must have been really worried about me as he had lost so much weight. He looked so tiny and slim. I was looking at him through puffy little slits for eyes. The fact it had only been a day was irrelevant. Then I was asleep again and I remained drowsy for quite some time. I needed blood transfusions, something, thankfully, that I had managed to escape during my two courses of chemotherapy. I have never felt so ill in all of my life. I can honestly say that if I could have closed my eyes and not opened them again at anytime during my life this would have been that moment. I have said before that I have been exhausted and zapped of all energy, but never to that extreme. I honestly felt that I wasn't going to make it. I recall Mr Schreuder coming in to check on me regularly, and when he came in I wanted to ask him if I was going to die, but I never got any further than saying "Mr Schreuder." I felt so weak.

The machines around me were beeping; I had doctor's checking me regularly and nurses with me constantly. On top of feeling absolutely terrible, I was back in the tropical temperature and incredibly hot, feeling so dehydrated and not allowed anything to drink. I was so thirsty my tongue felt it had shrivelled up to the back of my throat. By the evening I begged for some water and I was eventually given some tiny sponges to suck on by the nurses. I kept asking for more but they were closely monitoring the amount of fluid that I was taking and were restricting the amount given. Giles came back to see me that evening. I still wasn't that alert. I managed to communicate that I needed a drink and he returned with some more sponges for me to suck on. Night and day blurred into one under constant monitoring. The flap checked, blood pressure taken, various drips changed, more blood given, machine beeping constantly and I was still able to continue dozing.

By morning I was gasping for a drink. I would never survive a desert climate. Finally the doctors allowed me a whole cup of water. It was sheer heaven - the most refreshing drink ever. I was allowed another cup and I felt hydrated. I was so weak. I wanted to be put out of my misery. I was scared of feeling like that. Scared my children were going to lose me. I didn't even consider my surgery, I wanted to get better. I felt so ill. I have been told in the past that after surgery you may feel you've been hit by a bus, if this is the case I think I must have been hit by a bus three times over. Giles arrived. I was still so poorly. I needed another drink. With staff approval, Giles supplied another cup of water. Except now the water made me heave. It was from a machine - I could taste the chemicals in it. To take away the metallic taste, we were allowed to add some squash. Shortly afterwards, I was violently sick. That's why they were limiting the amount of fluid. Unable to sit up I was just vomiting where I lay. The nurses freshened me up and washed my hair with a dry shampoo. Then I fell asleep again. The nurses working in HDU are very attentive in major and a minor ways - they even took a photograph out of my bag of my girls and put it up for me for when I opened my eyes.

When I was stable I was taken from HDU and back to the ward and into my own room again. It was Friday evening, still feeling groggy; I was desperate to sleep my way through it. Giles was ecstatic to find me on the ward. He suggested that I phone Olivia and Annabel who would be pleased I was ok. My mum answered the phone and she understood that I couldn't really speak to her. I didn't have any strength. She passed the phone to Annie. I managed to ask her if she was having a lovely holiday. She was telling me about everything that she had been up to then asked me if I was having a lovely recovery in hospital. I managed to whisper to her that I was having a really lovely recovery. She repeated my answer to my mum. Some lovely recovery!

39

Worms on parachutes

I felt really weird that first evening on the ward. They may call it psychotic anaesthesia. Drugs have never been part of my life. Thankfully our paths have never collided. I experienced three days of hallucinations. I heard faint muffled voices swirling in my ears. I opened and closed my eyes frequently before realising that there was nothing and nobody there. The room was dark. The ward was on the eleventh floor and my bed sat in the middle of the room. I could see the street lights in the distance beneath me and I thought that those lights were silhouettes of people and watched as the passing cars ran everyone over; leaving their dead bodies slumped on the side of the road. The headlights made figures of giraffes and elephants trampling all over the victims. In the distance, I heard a TV and another patient was watching a motor Grand Prix. I sensed cars were racing all over my body, finally reversing up and down over my head. Maybe an unconscious sign of my inner determination to win, I thought afterwards, though I didn't experience a chequered flag.

But my most vivid, very repetitive and absolute memorable hallucination in such fine detail were the worms cascading from the ceiling in their hundreds, floating towards me attached to their parachutes before each and every one landed safely and delicately like feathers all over my body. They broke into song and dance as they happily touched down, wearing big white Elton John sunglasses. The watery muffled voices sounded so real and yet so unclear, and I kept seeing them. I felt nauseous with their floating motion and safe at the same time and I kept blinking to see if anymore were heading my way – they just kept falling.

Later, I remained fascinated with those images. I looked for messages – a meaning. *Worms on Parachutes* had always had me drawn as my title as soon as I wrote the paragraph. I researched what dreams mean – dreams are the nearest I could get to hallucinations. I actually found the association between worms and parachutes and how they come together in my very personal experience so spiritual and significant it actually sent shivers down my spine and every single hair on my body stand on end. From an interpretive internet site on 'what do your dreams mean', I found uncanny references:

To see worms indicates that you need to go deep into your unconsciousness in order to unearth your hidden feelings or desires. Alternatively worms symbolise little things that can be beneficial for your growth and well being. It also represents renewal. Perhaps you need to restore some aspect of yourself.

Then:

To dream about parachutes represents a protective force over you and you have a sense of security. If there were problems with the parachutes, for example they didn't open, it would suggest that you are let down by someone you relied on and trusted and would feel abandoned.

I can safely say that I never felt let down judging by the number of little worms that happily danced all over me, and not a parachute failed.

40

25 hour miracle man

It was Tuesday morning before I saw Mr Schreuder again. I watched him enter my room - close on six foot, dark hair which is slightly curly with a little grey interspersed, and glasses. Quite a young man considering the very senior position that he deservedly holds, quietly spoken with a soft South African accent and the most piercing and sincere eyes that totally draw you in and ooze *trust me I'm the surgeon*! I do not know how I managed to contain myself from crying. I had put so much trust in him and my life in his hands and he had been so determined and totally dedicated to ensure that he sculptured a reconstruction which was the best that he could do without failing again. He had found theatre challenging to say the least as I kept having blood clots and each time he stitched me up he wasn't satisfied, and he would start again. I think each member of the plastic department must have been involved in those twenty five hours at some stage - that is stamina and commitment. He is unquestionably the most talented person that I think I will ever have the pleasure of meeting after everything that he did for me. I guarantee that anyone who had shared my experience would, without hesitation, reach exactly the same conclusion and understand why he had won such a special place in our heart. I will always be truly grateful for his dedication to me and to the NHS that he serves. As a family, we are unbelievably proud of him. We nicknamed him Sir Fred! He was delighted with the result on examination: it must be hugely rewarding to see your skill, time and effort create such a perfect result, and to perceive the appreciation of your patient. My experience of the NHS has mostly been positive and I feel at times it is all too frequently undervalued. I'm not naive enough to think it is not without faults at all. When you receive outstanding care you should redress the balance - stand up and voice it in order to protect the service from unnecessary criticism and political interference.

My surgical drains had remained in for ten days. I really welcomed the stay in hospital. As my children were away, I didn't have anything to worry about at home so I was able to concentrate on true convalescence. Paradoxically, all of my friends went down with flu and heavy colds so they felt it was wise to stay away from me. All the rest I managed aided a quick recovery. I had felt so incredibly poorly but I've learnt when treated with respect the body has remarkable healing properties. Within days I was feeling much better. Not perfect but better would do.

The weather was glorious during my stay on Ward 11b. There was a balcony outside my room which I imagined was my own sun terrace as sunrays beamed through my windows. It was so warm I had visions of sitting outside on a sun lounger sipping a nice chilled glass of wine. Giles' arrival with a flask of my delicious thick green juice would just have to satisfy that craving for the moment. The wine would have to wait until I got home! I knew that I was building up a selection as friends, aware of my tastes, deposited bottles of Sauvignon Blanc or cava on my doorstep for my home-coming.

I was sent home twelve days later on a sunny Sunday afternoon, the day that Olivia and Annabel came home from Spain. They didn't arrive until the evening and I went home just after lunch. As I walked out of the hospital building into the natural sunlight I felt really strange after being cocooned on the ward. The light strained my eyes. I realised that I didn't have the strength that I originally thought. Looking back at the hospital, I felt strangely in awe of what I had been through and also what others had achieved for me. Although breast cancer has been an unpleasant intrusion into my life, it has also given me some very special lasting personal memories.

I looked forward to going home and was excited about seeing the girls later. Giles and I had the afternoon to ourselves, a perfect opportunity for a chilled glass of wine I'd been craving. The problem was I'd craved it for so long I actually couldn't stomach it when it was poured- the aromas were nauseating. Instead, it had to be a cup of tea and a *Hobnob* biscuit to dunk.

It was lovely having the kid's home that evening, looking healthy and sun kissed and full of exciting stories to share - they were so excited to see us. One day they might understand what I have been through but for now just to be at home, looking after them, was more than I could wish for. I have never wanted them to worry about me, opting to protect them. Childhood is so short lived and I want them to remember having a loving, happy childhood, not worrying about me ever being poorly or in hospital. I think that my children have been as unaffected as much as they could be and that is something that I am really proud of accomplishing.

Two days later I went back to hospital to have my dressings changed. When I was examined by the sister she was surprised to see that all my scarring had healed fantastically well and were all clean and dry and immediately discharged me from clinic, with a follow up appointment for six weeks later with Mr Schreuder. Remarkable to think that this had all healed in two weeks. It was perfect. I am still amazed at the skill of surgeons. I do believe that by actively helping myself played an important role in my healing and recovery. I might not have felt this when I woke up after twenty five hours of surgery but as the weeks and days went by I certainly did. The greatest piece of advice that I would give anyone going down this road would to ensure that they maintain a very healthy diet with lots of fruit and vegetables eaten as raw as possible with lean protein. It worked a treat for me!

41

I'll Breakthrough to make a breakthrough

Four weeks later I was back on the exercise regime. At first, I found walking caused me discomfort and I needed to take it very slowly. The nerves connected to the top of my thigh kept getting trapped, as all my tissue needed to knit back together. Although it was quite painful I was determined to complete the four mile circuit. I managed it in my own time. As time went by it started to get easier for me but it took a couple of months before I walked a great distance with ease again. It was now the end of June and whilst out walking in the fields I attempted a run, knowing that nobody could see me. After about ten steps I realised I was being far too optimistic – it was far too much for me as my bottom was now deprived of all physical sensation, completely numb and, just as before, it made me feel really nauseous on impact. Paradoxically, it was at that moment that I had my ingenious idea to enter the London Marathon for the following April. I needed something to aim at. I knew that I needed to push myself and set a challenge. Inspired by the wonderful medical team that I was very fortunate to have support me through all of my treatment, I decided to run for Breakthrough Breast Cancer. Breakthrough I feel is a positive charity that has successfully campaigned for better treatments and services. I am one of the sufferers who has benefited hugely from its endeavour and I wanted to give something back for everything that I have received. When I got home I immediately applied for a Golden Bond to run for Breakthrough and completed my application with all my supporting documentation. I was committed to raise £2000 and set out the ideas I had for raising it.

I can't really remember exactly how I felt when I submitted the request. I didn't think I was mad, or that I would never be able to do it, which is what a lot of people said to me when I mentioned what I was planning to do. They would be absolutely right. I could never contemplate starting to train for a marathon with such a negative mind set. You do have to remember that many people actually complete marathons with many challenges before them. Naturally Breakthrough was very happy to have me running for them. The greatest supporters that a charity will ever have are those supporters with a very personal story to tell, and they were keen to allocate me with one of their golden bonds! Now all I had to do was commit myself to a training regime and also find a way of raising the two thousand pounds. I was determined not to let anybody down, especially myself.

42

Marathon training

It was October when I discovered that I was running the marathon. By that stage I managed to run five kilometres a few times a week with slightly longer runs at the weekend. I have a lovely memory of running my first five kilometres and was really chuffed to have managed to do it. What made it extra special was to have Giles, Olivia and Annabel clapping me on in excitement as I completed the distance non-stop, shouting "come on mummy, you can do it."

In the months leading to Christmas I concentrated on building my fitness levels and then gradually increased the running distance. I quickly developed the stamina to run for an hour. My speed never improved but that wasn't my aim - I was happy being a plodder. My IPod Nano is the greatest gadget I have ever bought and acted as a great motivator, particularly when it congratulated me for completing my furthest distance, or my fasted mile. The latter didn't happen very often so I got a huge buzz on the occasions that it did, especially when I heard the voice in my ear of Lance Armstrong.

December came and we experienced the worst snow fall in a decade and left me in a state of panic as I then needed to work off plan, unable to get out on to the roads and pavements for fear of injuring myself on the ice. The kids, on the other hand, had never seen snow like it and were overcome with excitement, wrapping themselves up and going out to play on their sledges with friends, only appearing when they needed to warm themselves up and dry their clothes off while they sipped hot chocolate: cheeks glowing. It's what parents live for.

I had no alternative but to take to the garage and hit the treadmill for nearly three weeks. I even moved an old TV and managed to get hold of some cheesy chick flicks to pass away the boredom of staring at the four walls. *Pretty Woman*, my favourite film of all time - I have watched it over and over again, never tiring of it. But I must admit when you have a distance to run, the treadmill is so tedious and if I ever gave myself an opportunity to stop I never failed, completely defeating the object. It became apparent to me that I wasn't building my fitness and was desperate to return to the pavements when I felt safe doing so.

There is no easy way to haul yourself around a 26.2 mile circuit. You can't cheat and get out of the months of dedication, all the aching muscles and early morning runs come snow, rain, wind or shine and on the occasional days the exhaustion that your body feels from running every day. I had an advantage – I had already run a marathon in my mind; just getting myself through the treatment was perhaps part of the training in itself, the preparation that I needed to complete an endurance test of a lifetime. Naturally, I already possessed the determination.

The key to my training plan had to be clear, particularly as I wasn't in marathon running fitness shape at the start. I had a reason for running, though, and a real drive which was my focus and commitment: Breakthrough Breast Cancer and the ultimate motivator the race date, 25 April. There and then my plan was formulated in my mind. I knew exactly where I wanted to get to; I just needed to work out how I was going to get myself there.

Christmas and New Year had now come and gone and it was time to follow the stringent regime of my training plan and I needed to adhere to that religiously from that point on. I exercised every day in some capacity from jogging, swimming, walking and occasionally cycling. I had decided, foolishly, to follow a plan for a runner who aimed to complete the race in four hours. I was aware that that was way off my target but looking at all the other training plans that had been put together I felt I wouldn't be doing sufficient exercise for what I was now capable of. I chuckled to myself when I read the Sunday workout - go for a ten mile run! I knew that I couldn't possibly run ten miles at the moment and decided to see how far I could go without stopping. I managed a relatively proud eight miles, so I wasn't too far off. But I was absolutely shattered when I got home.

January's training went to plan and I was really delighted with how I progressed completely injury free and managed a very do-able ten miles, my first hurdle!

The snow decided to make another appearance in February and again I needed to get back to the treadmill and grin and bear my way through the increased distances, all the time chanting to myself that I could do it and get through the boredom, and this time I didn't allow myself to stop or slow the speed button. I was now in the zone. The focus and tunnel vision just engulfed me more than anything and the power of my mind is what carried me on. When you have got something to do you just have to get on and do it. My mind was now functioning mechanically almost like a robot, programmed to keep going and carry on.

Back out to the pavement the cold, frosty, foggy mornings didn't really bother me too much, almost becoming oblivious to the weather as it was a minor affect to my training. Some mornings I felt the cold really burn my chest as I took every deep breath, but I knew that would subside after twenty minutes and I would be ready to start stripping off. I hated getting too hot anyway and always ended up running in a vest top, with my jacket tied around my waist.

February and early March went amazingly well for me. I was even lucky to plan a week in Spain at the end of February to help me acclimatise to running in warmer weather conditions. On arrival in Spain we realised that just like home, Spain was experiencing adverse weather conditions as well. I had visions of running along the promenade as soon as the sun rose, with the water lapping along the shore as I took every step breathing in the fresh air of the Mediterranean as I clocked up the miles every day. Instead, each morning I ran through deep puddles and sea mist and torrential rain, determined to complete my planned fourteen miles. When we returned home I felt like a real Olympic athlete - it was great! The long runs on the Sunday morning were the best. I bounced out of bed at seven o'clock, got dressed and then I was out of the front door straight away. As soon as the door closed behind me I focused on the job in hand; and then towards the end of my run I looked forward to getting home to indulge in a hot Sunday roast, enjoying my roast potatoes and not feeling guilty about eating them, followed by my favourite dessert of all time, rhubarb crumble and custard, then a well deserved rest on the sofa to get over the exertion of the morning.

However, getting over the fifteen mile hurdle was incredibly tough for me and I struggled on those important Sunday morning runs. One week I had absolutely nothing in me at all and no matter how hard I tried to concentrate and focus, I just couldn't. I needed to stop half a dozen times and eventually gave in and went home and cried. I told Giles that I just couldn't do it; it was all going wrong for me now. I got in the bath and for some reason my whole face ached. I didn't know if it was my head, my neck or what ached, but I just couldn't do anything with myself.

Ironically my legs and feet were great, and weren't giving me any cause for concern, apart from the couple of toe nails that I seemed to lose on a regular basis. I tried to put out of my mind my paranoia and thought that I now had a brain tumour and the constant jolting and shaking of my head triggered something off. But I only experienced that on my longer runs.

As the final weeks to my training started to draw to a close I wasn't in the position that I initially hoped I would be. I had definitely done too much too early but I still needed to stretch out the distance, and now time was against me. I couldn't allow for any more unsuccessful Sunday mornings and I needed to hit at least eighteen miles before race day. Giles knew that I was fading fast. He always knew the route that I took on the longer runs, and he obviously knew what speed I ran at and once I had hit the seventeen mile point, he drove out to see me with the girls in the car, windows down as they approached me, clapping and shouting great words of encouragement,

"You're doing great mummy; well done you're looking strong!" Yep, I have produced some great liars! But it gave me that huge burst of energy that I was just so lacking, and made me hit my eighteen point one miles which is the furthest distance recorded on my IPod Nano to this day.

But the pain in my head was now worsening and I just didn't know what to do with myself as soon as I stopped running. Painkillers weren't dulling the pain and I was up all night rocking in agony, until it dawned on me that it was my teeth. Completely neglected for the last three years as my dentist was way up there with anaesthetists for me. I avoid them unless in an absolute emergency. And I had an emergency. The marathon was at the end of the following week. Great, I had an abscess, needed root canal treatment and a cap. Relief, not quite the brain tumour I originally thought and all sorted out in ultra efficient time, giving me twelve days to concentrate on the job in hand.

That weekend, my final long run under my belt complete, I felt strong again and ready for the week that lay ahead for me. That week we were hit with a heat wave. Brilliant, I've never run in warm weather conditions and hadn't had any practice as it had been a really harsh winter. Even a trip to Spain in late February dealt us a week of continuous rain and winds, not the lazy days we were so looking forward to. I had no idea how I would cope in the heat. I had prepared for eventualities but the weather was obviously beyond the control of all the prospective runners. I had done my best. I had to be philosophical - what will be, will be. Or *que sera, sera* - as I had learned in Malaga.

So forget about all of the physical challenges. The most important rule, I told myself, was to remain positive, always keep motivated and never to forget the cause. I always told myself that I could do it, and I know I broke on occasions but this has also been an incredible learning curve as my character was tested. I have really told myself how strong I am and how much I have within me, and how important it is to simply block out all negative thoughts.

43

I can now fill a bra but can I fill the collection can?

I have never been directly involved or responsible for any fundraising activity, so venturing into this field really filled me with dread. One of the biggest obstacles that I faced was feeling that I was begging for money for myself, and not taking it too personally when individuals preferred to abstain. I understand more than most that the public will support charities that mean something to them or perhaps that they have had a personal encounter themselves.

We faced a tough economic climate so raising money was always going to be challenging, bordering on tough. I needed to raise two thousand pounds! Just as important as raising that much money was also in lifting levels of awareness of breast cancer locally, especially in a younger age group.

To begin, I set up my Just Giving page. That was quick and easy, even for me, and immediately enabled me to reach out to a huge influential audience. Supporters made their donations, without me then having the embarrassment of going round collecting the money when I completed the run. I set up my page in the November and promoted it on Facebook. That acted as a huge platform to launch myself from and allowed me to access a section of people that I would not have been able to connect with by any other means. In the beginning, donations came in very slowly, but I didn't allow that to distract me. Instead I kept reposting my page to remind people why I felt it was so important to support the cause. In actual fact, with the number of times I made my pledge I don't think they could ever forget what I wanted to achieve, as this disease is terrifying and is still taking too many victims.

I wasn't overly confident that just having a Just Giving page was going to deliver what I needed it to. I then needed to think creatively. I needed to take myself out into the community and promote what I was doing and why I was doing it. That's when I produced a flyer which I put through every door in my home village with the harsh reality of what breast cancer is and just how many people are affected by it daily. I added a little photograph of myself with a great beaming smile, looking the absolute pillar of health. Almost a statement – we can fight this together. It was a success and the donations started coming in, names I didn't recognise, the reconfirmation that so many people have been affected at some stage in their life.

Still not entirely satisfied, I needed to come up with a series of events that would appeal to everyone living locally. People don't mind parting with money if they are going to have a good time, or a pleasant afternoon, or for the men, a round of golf and a bacon butty to keep them happy. So with the ever appreciative help of friends, An Afternoon Tea Party in our village hall, a Pink Party in the local pub, and a game of golf at a local golf club were all diarised, all we needed to do was get busy planning them.

With the venues quickly reserved for various dates, in the background I immediately started contacting local businesses to try and obtain raffle and auction prizes to increase the interest so more people would support me at whichever event they chose to attend. The prospect of contacting companies filled me with dread in the initial stages as I faced possible rejection. I should never have felt that fear as every single person that I approached was incredibly obliging and sincerely wanted to support Breakthrough Breast Cancer. My contacts were local restaurants, hairdressers, florists, wine merchants, golf clubs, even a handy man wanted to donate a couple of days work to carry out any DIY project that anyone requested. Even friends working in large retail organisations donated large luxury items. It didn't really take us that long before we had a very credible list of gifts to offer, from leather purses and handbags, to a flat screen TV and digital camera, to tickets for popular sporting events.

Anyone for Tea

The Afternoon Tea Party kicked off our first fundraising event, held on a wet Saturday afternoon. It was organised by a friend and a former neighbour, who wanted me to concentrate on my training and not worry about anything else. All they asked was that I turn up on the afternoon to enjoy it. What we did agree at the outset was for everyone who came along to feel like they were being treated to tea at The Ritz.

As I walked into the village hall I was met by an array of pink, balloons, table cloths and napkins. All the tables had been set out and were laid with cups and saucers and sugar bowls. Everyone was served tea at their tables and my girls amongst some of their friends volunteered to be waitresses for the afternoon and walked around with trays filled with the widest variety of cakes on each, which were all homemade and had been baked and happily donated by people living within the village. Everyone had an unlimited amount to eat and drink.

The hall was filled with supporters all afternoon, whilst outside we still had people patiently queuing in the pouring rain. There was a huge buzz as people just came together from all the community to enjoy the event. I'm sure that they walked away having thoroughly enjoyed themselves but also in the knowledge that they had supported a worthy cause. We raised over six hundred and fifty pounds – an incredible effort for a cup of tea and a slice of cake. An amount that also meant I had exceeded my promised pledge.

Golf Day

I'm sure the impact of what Giles has been through in his own way has affected him. He has always maintained a brave, very positive attitude towards me, but I know it has been difficult for him at times and our friends have always been there for him. Breast cancer also affects men so it was important to profile the disease amongst them. The week after the tea party the boys took to the golf course to take part in a charity golf day. They were met with bacon rolls and coffee on arrival to set them up for a competition that was always going to be incredibly fierce! Before they were allowed to step foot onto the green they needed to part with some more money and purchase some raffle tickets in exchange for a golf cap courtesy of New Era. The raffle prizes consisted of all golfing equipment, bags, trolleys, clubs and putters all kindly donated to us to maximise on our fundraising opportunity on the day. The raffle was drawn at the end of the golf when they all relaxed and enjoyed a sandwich and a well earned pint, as they waited in anticipation the announcement of the winner!

Going One, Going Twice, SOLD

The Pink Party, such an original name I know, also consisted of an auction and raffle and completed all of my planned events. We advertised this locally and was planned for the afternoon after the golf. As the day approached I panicked as I felt we had insufficient items for put into our auction lot. Giles continually reminded me that I needed to be more confident, we had plenty and not to worry. I just wanted to end on a successful and enjoyable event.

In my mind I had the perfect person to orchestrate the auction, and I knew that he would hold the attention of everyone in the pub and create a huge amount of excitement especially as alcohol was going to be consumed. He had a natural auctioneers chant, natural charm and humour and would really rise to the challenge.

The party was open to all and the ticket price consisted of a carvery as well. Like every event I never really knew how successful it was going to be or if indeed anyone would turn up. Confidence is not one of my strongest traits.

So after getting up really early and running sixteen miles I returned home to get ready for the party and had a glass of wine which I needed to help calm my nerves. I even managed to blow up dozens of balloons after running that distance! I planned to decorate the pub and make it pink and atmospheric

Fundraising comes down to a joint effort and I have been fortunate enough to have people around me that have stepped in to help me when I have needed them the most. So when my friend volunteered to sell the raffle tickets for me on the afternoon I was absolutely delighted. I was more than happy to fade into the background.

It was a beautiful spring day and the sun had been shining all day. The doors to the pub were wide open and the pub was filled with family and friends and all the regulars, some of whom I have never met before. All the ladies chose to wear an item of pink. Everyone around me was drinking but in my mind I just tried to take everything in.

Robbie, the auctioneer, started to take control and stepped up to the microphone and was immediately in his element as he got the auction underway. He had such a magical chant that ensured bids were coming immediately and were being raised. I remember we had some football tickets to a Premier league match in a lot that were going for a hundred pounds one minute and suddenly the bid finished at seven hundred and sixty pounds. It was surreal and crazy.

My favourite lot had to be one of my proudest moments to date. Olivia wanted to sing for me and stood up in her little pink tutu and leggings, and in full view of everyone in the pub sang her favourite song at the time, "Hallelujah" by Alexandra Burke. She sang it beautifully, and ensured that she got every single verse out to a massive round of applause.

A friend had bid one hundred and eighty pounds for her to sing and the pub did a quick whip round and collected a further two hundred pounds. Some of them had not realised that Olivia was only nine. That had to be the pinnacle of my fundraising attempts, and I'm sure that Olivia will remember her moment for the rest of her life.

By the time the raffle was drawn and the auction over, copious amounts of alcohol drunk everyone around me was laughing, chatting amongst themselves, dancing, and having a ball. It then dawned on me that the afternoon had raised a very respectable five thousand, five hundred pounds – an amazing figure that also reinforced my conviction that lots of people want to support the cause. We continued to dance the night away and at midnight I collected all of the balloons, went out into the car park, looked up into the star filled sky and released all of the balloons into the air as tears streamed down my face. I looked into the stars and mouthed thank you. I realised how lucky I was. What a day it had been and I returned to the bar to join Giles for a quick night cap

But it had been a long day and I was ready for bed so I left my drink on the bar, dragged Giles away from his friends to home and bed, my head just buzzed with the excitement of the day, ecstatic to achieve an amount of money that was going to benefit so many people, but conscious more than ever that I could never let these people down and not complete the Marathon. I couldn't have asked for anything more and I'm glad that everyone who wanted to be involved had been.

44

Pink all the way

We organised for a pink limousine to take us all to London on the Saturday morning before the Marathon. I wanted the kids to have a treat to add to their memories of the whole experience and to make it a special weekend for them. They are, after all, the most important aspect of my life and everything that I do is ultimately for them. They gave me so much encouragement and make absolutely everything worth fighting for. The pink Hummer turned into our road at nine o'clock in the morning. The limo company had decided to give us an upgrade as I was running for Breakthrough and the lady that we had booked it with had also been successfully treated for breast cancer. It was quite an offensive fluorescent pink Hummer and I would have preferred a rather more pastel shade if I am honest. The girls loved it and thoroughly enjoyed travelling down the M1 to the big city in it. They chuckled and pretended to drink champagne and waved at all the passing cars on the way. The roads weren't busy and we reached our hotel, The Lancaster London, quickly. Even so, it is a journey that will forever be engrained in my memory – it took me to one of my greatest achievements to date of my life.

Our hotel was situated right opposite Hyde Park and as soon as we had dropped off our luggage we made our way to the park for a walk, a coffee and an ice-cream. The weather remained warm – conditions I didn't enjoy for running. The park was filled with all sorts of people, men with bare chests playing football, lots of mature ladies going for their morning stroll, tourists, runners kitted out in all their gear looking immaculate coupled with having great running styles. As Giles and I sat over coffee, I chattered: *do I run like that? am I as slow as her? does my bum look like that when I'm running? I wish I looked like her - do you think I will ever look like that if I carry on running?* In the end he told me to shut up and enjoy my coffee. Afterwards, we made our way to Kensington Palace to look around the beautiful manicured gardens. It was where Princess Diana had lived and the girls were intrigued when I told them that I had been privileged to meet her. I had studied business and finance with travel and tourism at Aylesbury College. Princess Diana visited the college and paid particular interest to the travel and tourism department. I remember our class wearing our business uniform that day, a navy suit with a white blouse and big red bow. Then, as Princess Diana entered our classroom, she came to my bank of desks where I sat with my friends and enquired how we felt about working with the public. We had our photographs taken for the local newspaper. "Really mummy?" they said, impressed, and started quizzing me for more details as we continued to admire the beautiful gardens.

From there we went to Harrods in a black cab, and later a tour of the sights on an open top city tour bus, allowing the girls to see Downing Street, Buckingham Palace, the Houses of Parliament, St Paul's Cathedral, and The Mall. I tried to imagine what I would feel like running down this route in the morning but I just couldn't identify with that. I had no idea what the following day would have in store for me.

It was almost like a picture postcard, taking in all the sights in the glorious sunshine. London looked the perfect cosmopolitan city for which is it renowned, vibrant with people from all over the world, the cafe and wine bars filled with customers becoming a pavement society.

We closed our day at Pizza Express having a pasta meal, which everyone tells you to do prior to any run. I had a really enjoyable day but I had spent the majority of it feeling incredibly nervous and anxious for the following day. My stomach churned and when my meal arrived I couldn't stomach eating and only picked at it in between the occasional sip of water - which was equally as important.

We all knew that we couldn't be late to bed that night as we needed to make our way to Greenwich Park early in the morning. We headed back to the hotel shortly after our meal. By this time the nerves were seriously taking their toll on me, coupled with the premature arrival of the time of the month. Great. Just what I needed. An added factor that I hadn't considered and certainly didn't need when I had the distance to run. The immediate zap in energy levels. Back in the hotel room I got everything ready for the morning and put the chip onto my trainer laces – a device to record my finish time, and pinned my number to my Breakthrough running top. Then I ran a hot bath to try and relax and told myself that all I could do was my best. I didn't have any time to beat but had an idea that following my training runs and half marathon time I roughly estimated that I should finish in five hours and thirty minutes. I based this on my half time averaging two hours and twenty eight minutes. A fatal error that first time marathon runners make, underestimating their finish time. As I got into bed that night I sensed that I was not going to have a great night's sleep. The hotel room was hot, London was very noisy, not like the quiet village where I lived, and my mind was just too active to switch off. The girls were really excited for me and Giles told me how proud he was of me. I didn't get a wink of sleep that night. I must have checked my watch fifteen times before I decided to get up at four o'clock and run another bath, which I managed to lie in for an hour. As I lay in the bath, I reflected on the last year.

I couldn't believe that just exactly twelve months previously I had woken from a lengthy operation that had left me feeling life was zapped from me and where I could have just closed my eyes forever to escape what

I felt. Now I was absolutely full of the zest for life and really wanted to perform as a tribute to all those people who had made it possible. As I dressed and put on my running top it was hard to grasp that I was there running for Breakthrough Breast Cancer. I just didn't seem like the person standing before me in the mirror: the person who in just three years had been diagnosed with breast cancer, had undergone rigorous chemotherapy, lost everything that had defined her as a woman, had three lengthy operations, got herself fit, lost weight, trained for a marathon, organised fundraising events for the cause, and here I was about to run the London Marathon. In some ways it probably wasn't until that day that I finally realised what a journey I had been on. I am positive most of the time; in my reformed and reinvigorated self I am proud to emerge confident in myself and always touched by gratitude towards those who helped me in big and small ways. In physical appearance, nobody would ever be able to tell the difference – a tribute to those surgical, medical and nursing specialists. I really did have miracle people working for me. I was very lucky to stumble across that team of professionals. The biggest inspiration I had to ever consider running the marathon was that very team of people around me, those people who absolutely got me through it so graciously.

45

Race Day: 25 April

I had planned my breakfast for the morning. Weetabix with a banana and I looked forward to it. As I entered the breakfast room I immediately mingled with the other runners having their breakfast. Unfortunately, there wasn't any Weetabix, so I chose my next favourite cereal, Muesli. As I sat down with my bowl and a glass of water, I immediately felt sick again, but I knew that I needed to force myself to eat. As I put a spoon of Muesli into my mouth, it was like sawdust. I chewed and chewed but I just couldn't swallow it, no matter how hard I tried. So my breakfast consisted of a cup of tea with half a sugar.

It was still early and as I looked out on to Hyde Park from the restaurant it didn't look as hot as forecast, which was quite reassuring. When I got back up to the room, Olivia and Annabel were dressed in their pink leggings, a white T-shirt with a pink ribbon on the front, pink jackets and black and pink baseball caps and we made our way to Greenwich Park with all of the other competitors. The furthest place that we could go together were the gates entering the park so it was here that we said our goodbyes and good luck. Olivia presented me with a card that she had made for me with the following poem that she had written inside it.

Mummy's Marathon Poem

To someone with great style,
I'm with you every mile,
You are an inspiration,
Who's had lots of operations,
You are a mother of two,
Who really love you,
I adore you and other people do too!
I love you mummy,
And this is a poem just for you.

The look of excitement on the girls' faces is something that will remain with me: that look of *we don't know what you are going to do but we know it's going to be great!* They looked so proud and in some ways so innocent to my reasons for taking part and raising the level of funds that we had. I want their future and the future of many others to be free of the fear of everything that I have been through. Then they watched me walk through the gates and into the park and they would see me again on Tower Bridge at the halfway mark.

This is the day that I had focused on through the winter months. I had been blown away with the level of support that I had been so lucky to receive and the amount of money that was raised for a cause that I believe is going to shape the way for the future. Now I only had one simple thing do and that was to complete the twenty six miles and three hundred and eighty five yards. Then I would be worthy of raising the ten thousand, two hundred and eighty nine pounds and fifteen pence. The benefits of raising that level of money go without saying. But I did, however, feel an enormous amount of pressure which I just quietly carried on my shoulder. There was absolutely no way that I could fail my supporters or give into the occasional few who had doubted that I could ever do it. Those people do exist irrespective of what you may go through.

As soon as I walked into the park I could feel the buzz of everyone and the loud up beat music was really motivating and added to the excitement of the whole event. I was more worried about finding the right lorry to unload all my belongings on to which would then find me on the other side. But of course arrangements for the London Marathon are down to a fine art and attention to detail spot on and I found the lorry with ease. Then the next stop were the toilets which I hadn't heard great reviews on but as I was early they were spotlessly clean and furthermore there were not any queues.

46

Pen 9

Now I was ready and able to relax more. The place was packed with runners though I managed to spot the Breakthrough runners - we were all running in the same designed vests. There was great camaraderie amongst us all as we wished each other luck and exchanged our reasons for running for Breakthrough. When I looked around me, I realised how many people are affected not just by breast cancer but other forms of cancer and life threatening illnesses, and those inspirational people who live each day with challenges in their way. Each and every one of those runners had a very personal reason for running. It is a moment that puts life into perspective. It's when people have photos of their loved ones that have lost their fight that hits you the most, and it brings tears to your eyes. I don't know if it was my brain working properly but somehow I managed to detach myself from my feelings and switch off to anything that I was unable to cope with. That was until I got myself into Pen 9 for the start of the run. Everyone was running for a charity in this pen and there were two young ladies in front of me who were running in memory of their mum with her photograph on their running tops. It was at that point that I realised how ill prepared I was. I had completed my training plan down to the T and followed everything that I should have done. I knew that I could physically have done no more. But I underestimated the most powerful influence of all: suddenly I wasn't as strong as I should have been. It's the mind. The emotion, the heart-tugging, throat-choking feelings that engulf you. Instead of thinking 'great' on those ladies on the start line doing something positive in memory of their mum, I immediately thought how they could be Olivia and Annabel. I choked on tears. No level of training could ever have prepared me for that. I needed to refocus quickly. I had received the best treatment, I had survived and there I was about to run the Virgin London Marathon. Something that I never considered three years previously.

Somewhere between all the aggressive treatment and the lengthy operations that my body had been subjected to for the last few years emerged an incredible strength that had grown within me and that was the person that I needed to connect with and get focused. Nobody and nothing could take away what I have achieved and overcome.

The etiquette in the marathon is to line up with groups of runners that will run at the same pace as you. Probably like most runners, though, I got myself to the front of Pen 9, just so I did not start right at the back. Richard Branson officially started the race as it was the first Virgin London

Marathon. The last time I saw him was at a launch party for the Virgin Airlines London to Johannesburg route. Then everyone started moving. There were so many stampeding footsteps, although we moved pretty slowly to begin with. My race didn't officially start until the chip which was attached to my trainer lace crossed the start line. Having only ever run on my own previously I was aware of the presence of all the other runners around me and was aware that they were all running at a much faster pace than me. I remember approaching the first mile marker and I looked up at the clock above it. I couldn't understand how I had run the first mile so slowly. I found it really off putting. I started to focus purely on the time which in hindsight was just ridiculous. I was such an inexperienced runner that I was totally oblivious that the timers were set from the very first runner crossing the line. By the time I hit the four mile marker I was completely deflated and questioned what was going so wrong for me. I had never been this slow in any of my training runs. I then started to calculate the time that I would reach Giles and the girls and my friends. They were all at Tower Bridge which was roughly the half way mark. Giles is a very competitive person and I felt that he would be disappointed with me and my time when I got to him. I also had visions of the girls getting really bored as they watched all the other runners whilst they waited to see me.

It was quite early into the race that I witnessed the first casualties of the testosterone brigade. The guys who just ran off far too quickly and then wondered why they collapsed so early on. It was quite a concerning sight with their oxygen masks on and in agony. I definitely didn't want to end up like them so I decided at the six mile mark to just continue plodding along and to make it to the finish line. It was at that point that I clocked my first supporters, Danny and Emma. Seeing people that you know supporting you really lifts your spirits and reinforces that determination that you start lacking.

It was inevitable that I would be overtaken by the masses, but I really did have to chuckle to myself when the rhino overtook me and before I knew it another followed. I thought to myself that I didn't remember overtaking the rhino earlier but then it dawned on me that there were a number of runners running for the charity 'Save the Rhino'. Rhinos always featured in my life as a child when we would go out to the bush for a weekend away. I remember my dad getting out of the car to take photographs of wildlife and suddenly from nowhere would appear rhino's behind us. My dad always had to make a sharp leap back into the car and slowly drive off so not to aggravate them too much. Then there I was being overtaken by them throughout my run.

During my training I had run with my I-pod listening to some really pumping running songs until two weeks before the marathon someone told me not to run to music. Just to take everything from the crowds because they would really spur you on and get you through the distance.

I took that advice on board, rather foolishly. It was the biggest mistake I made. Not only did I not have my music to listen to but I didn't even think about taking it just in case I needed a little motivation and distraction on my way. Even though the streets were paved with thousands of supporters spurring you on, steel bands playing, and bands playing '*Living on a Prayer*', as young children handed out sweets and chocolates when you really needed them, this, if I'm honest, just wasn't enough for me to get me through. I really needed my *'YMCA,' 'Girls just wanna have Fun'& 'Uptown Girl'* to name a few to take my mind off my running and to allow the time to pass much quicker.

All I had to focus on instead of my music were the mile markers obviously located to highlight each mile run. After passing the markers I instantly thought that there must be another marker in a minute, but instead the distance between each one just seemed to get greater and greater. If I had been at home I would have happily listened to four or five songs and before I knew it I would have ranked up another mile, but there on the streets of London and in full view of all the spectators I just had to conclude to myself that the miles in London must just be longer than the miles in Bedfordshire.

At twelve miles I felt the excitement as I approached Tower Bridge where lots of supporters congregated in the hope to catch a glimpse of the family or friend that they were supporting. The pubs were open and the crowds with beers in their hands, cheered us on. I spotted my brother and my pace picked up as I wanted him to be proud of me and not see the struggle that I was feeling. Instantly I got that sudden burst of energy that I was so desperate for to get me over the bridge where I knew the remaining supporting army waited in great anticipation and excitement. I turned the corner and immediately caught glimpse of my little supporters, Olivia and Annabel, in their bright pink leggings screaming as they clocked me. I draped my arms around them and Giles and burst into tears. I told Giles how tough it was and even mentioned that I didn't think that I was going to be able to finish it. It just wasn't happening for me today. In training I would have just put it down to having a bad run as you get those days, believe me. But that day I knew that it was tough going all the way and on reflection I would actually classify it as my worst performance and furthermore it would be the only run where people would actually ask me what time I did it in! So ridiculously I also started to feel a sense of embarrassment. When I set out to do anything I always set out to do my best and my best just wasn't happening today.

With the clock against me I still needed to soldier on. I had reached the half way mark. Only the same to do again, I told myself. Miraculously, I seemed fine for the next three miles and felt quietly smug when I started to overtake a few runners. I had reached 16 miles, slowly I know without any blisters or aches and didn't need to take advantage of the Vaseline on offer, which others grabbed in the handfuls to put in between their thighs or wherever it was needed. I started chatting to a lady who was running for Cancer Research UK and she was really struggling with chaffing and was grabbing the Vaseline in bucket loads. She was so determined not to give up because of all the money that she had raised for her charity. I asked her casually how much she had managed to raise and she told me seven hundred and fifty pounds, as she was trying to get hold of some more Vaseline. Anybody who puts themselves in a position to raise any level of funds for charity should be saluted because it is the most selfless thing that you can do and it heightens awareness of the cause. Furthermore fundraising is hard as there are so many charities out there that need vital funds and you have to be selective as you cannot possibly support all of them. It did, however, make me think of the amount of money that Breakthrough would benefit from by me running the marathon and I needed to complete the course to allow myself to feel worthy of raising such a huge amount of money. I had to plod on and leave her behind and just get to The Mall.

So I left the bleakness of The Isle of Dogs behind me, with the nauseating smell of burgers' and sausages which people were barbecuing on the side of the roads. Canary Wharf wasn't that much better as I hit the twenty mile mark. The furthest distance that I have ever covered in one go, and boy did I know it, when every step that I took became agony. It felt each time I lifted my leg to take a step my hip bone was knocked out of its socket, and when I put my foot down it was being placed back into its socket. The pain reduced me to tears and I saw the St Johns Ambulance service and I really wanted to give myself up and amble my way towards them, but I had hit twenty miles, I only had six and a bit to go.

I could do it - trying to convince myself. But I was right. I needed to finish it properly and I would never forgive myself if I didn't. After all, the pain wasn't that bad. It certainly didn't compare with having an I-gap procedure and trying to sit on the toilet for the first time following the operation when you didn't know whether it was better to sit down slowly, sliding down the hand rail, or just to fall on the toilet seat and suffer the consequences of the intense stinging and burning sensation. That is painful but at a completely different level. So the tears came and passed and up through the tunnel I emerged to see my little supporters again still screaming and full of the carnival atmosphere. Big hugs and kisses were exchanged and I was on the twenty three mile marker. It would soon be over. My hips never did recover for the rest of the race and slowly I reached the twenty four miles. The crowds started to lessen as the main runners had finished and there were just a few hangers on cheering for you, telling you how well you'd done you're nearly there now, not long, keep going. The best part of the run came when I completely missed the twenty five mile marker and suddenly I was on twenty six miles. I was there on The Mall, only another three hundred and eighty five yards to go, and I'd done it.

But just when you think it's over those three hundred and eighty five yards are a killer. Forget the twenty six miles that go before it. There I was, the finish line well within reach, my brother and his family in the Grandstands, and finally I was there, across the line, and finally, in relief, a smile on my face. I'd done it and a medal around my neck as recognition for completing it. Thank you family, friends, my medical team and Breakthrough Breast Cancer - you gave me an incredible memory and a great personal achievement I would have never thought possible. In my working career, Richard Branson placed his arms over my shoulders for a photograph as part of a Virgin Airlines promotion (I still have it); sorry, Sir Richard, by a million miles (or at least 26 of them) I'd rather have the Virgin medal for completing the marathon on behalf of the cause I believed in – and all the causes that thousands of runners are prepared to literally lay down their lives for every year.

London Marathon 25.04.10

We've seen you Sarah on our travels
Pounding through streets
and running through puddles
There was no let up when the snow came
You jumped on the treadmill
and put us to shame
Your reason for this to reach your goal

And finish the marathon, what a brave soul
When you crossed the line, weary and sore
You know it was worth it for such a good cause
Now it's all over get lots of rest
But most of all enjoy your success.

*By **Kathryn and Graeme***

I actually put the following message on my just giving page a couple of days later:

Thanks for taking the time to visit my Just Giving page once again!

Thank you so much for all of your support in helping me to raise an enormous amount of money for Breakthrough Breast Cancer. When all of the money is collected we would have raised a total amount of £10,289, WOW!!!

All I can say about Sunday is that I crossed the line with a huge smile on my face, a medal round my neck, injury free, (except for the loss of three toe nails!) and the knowledge that I had raised an amount of money that certainly surpassed all of my expectations.

The emotions of the day were something that I could not have prepared myself for, and there were certainly some very dark moments on the marathon route. I have to say, though, that the crowds were completely amazing with everyone cheering you on and there was a real carnival atmosphere. The streets were just paved with supporters handing out sweets, chocolates, even sandwiches to anybody that needed them. I however felt incredibly sick nearly all the way round so chose to decline every offer, just for a change!

By the 19 mile mark, the pain really kicked in and the seizures and stiffening started. At every mile point there was a St John's Ambulance Brigade crew and I could have so easily withdrawn from the race and handed myself over to them, but there was absolutely no way that I could have let everyone down who has shown their support, but most importantly I would have been so disappointed in myself and so full of regret if I had allowed myself to withdraw.

So instead I finished proudly (NOT) in six hours and forty five minutes, still beating Katie Price's time last year of seven hours fifteen minutes. But I achieved what I set out to do:

To simply raise the awareness of Breast Cancer locally and especially amongst younger women as this illness can strike anyone. So please check yourselves regularly, and if in doubt check it out. The earlier the diagnosis the greater the chance of successful treatment, and ultimately survival!

You will be pleased to know that this is the last time you will see this page as I am now retiring from marathon running. One runner on the course said to me that there are two types of marathon runners, one just get the bug and keep going back for more, and the other do it the once and never again. I certainly know which one I fall into. I will never ever put myself through that experience again, but I will take it forward with me through life, and remember it as one of my greatest achievements. Through every negative experience comes a positive one!

Once again thank you.xxx

47

My greatest loss

With all of the focus of the marathon training behind me I felt a real void and emptiness. I have learned through this whole experience that I need to continually plan some challenge or I am increasingly aware that I start to spend too much time thinking about what I have been through and my mood very quickly dips. For a couple of months I reverted to power walking as I am not good at running during the warmer months. I actually really enjoyed it again. I promised the girls that following my final operation, when I knew that everything would be complete and I would be in the best possible health, we could get a little dog to complete the Phillips home. Something that they had been begging for, for some time, but there was always that 'what if' in my mind. I also needed to make sure that we chose the right dog and breed. It would also be company for me when I am out walking as my reasons for walking were to keep myself as fit as I could to get me through surgery and with all of that behind me I would still have a reason to continue.

The week that followed the marathon I returned to the Lister Hospital to see Mr Schreuder to discuss the final stages of my reconstructive surgery. He still needed to remove the fullness from the outer side of the my initial reconstruction and he advised me that he would remove this and some scar tissue surgically and then he would go ahead and do the nipple reconstruction at the same time. I tried to beg him to do it under a local anaesthetic and not a general one, but he really wasn't in the mood to negotiate. As he wanted to make sure that I was happy with the positioning of the nipples he gave me some little round plasters to use to mark where I wanted the nipples to be placed. I needed to stick them on the morning of surgery. I giggled and the look on my face must have said it all. As if I was going to play pin the nipple on the Freddy tum bums. Secondly if I had left this to Giles, goodness knows where they would have ended up on me and let's face it, Mr Schreuder is the professional. He's done it all before and knows exactly where to place them so I decided to leave it all up to him.

I woke up on the morning of my final procedure that would restore my body to its original glory as best as it possibly could be. I was as ready as I was ever going to be and as it was only a minor procedure I decided to drive myself to hospital leaving Giles at home with the girls to get them ready for school. I felt relatively calm driving to Lister Hospital, although as I drove closer to Stevenage and caught sight of the tall hospital building in the distance my stomach trembled. As I parked my car I felt really nauseous. Walking back into the hospital to undergo a procedure just bought all the memories flooding back. This was the very place that I had felt so ill the previous year, and I would be heading to the same theatre all over again. I started panicking and having heart palpitations. I had walked down the main hospital corridor so many times in the last twelve months as I attended various out-patient appointments, but the walk that morning felt different. I almost felt emotionally unresponsive and I don't know how I managed to get myself to the admissions ward, where I was ushered into a consulting room on arrival. It was there, like all the other mornings on my theatre days that I waited for Mr Schreuder and his registrar to arrive. I sat there rocking with fear and nerves – I must have looked like a mad woman as the nurses kept coming in to me and asking me if I was alright. Why do they tell you that having the nipple reconstruction is like the cherry on top of the cake? It almost felt like you were not perfect until that was done, but actually I did want it doing and after everything else that I had been through, this was nothing dramatic. I never envisaged that I would feel that fearful of having such a small procedure and being put out to sleep for such a short amount of time. *I was about to have the smallest operation to date, why was I in pieces over it?* I kept asking myself.

Mr Schreuder walked on to the ward with his registrar and visited all of his patients scheduled on his theatre list that day. I knew he had arrived before I heard him speak.

Over time I became conscious that I now recognised every consultant who treated me simply by their footsteps. The sound of their shoes as the heels clipped the polished surface of the floor with every step they took. In fact if they all walked before me in an identity parade today, I would recognise each and every one of them, blind-folded. I felt my palpitations worsen as I lost control of my breathing pattern and started to hyperventilate and panic. Then he made his entrance in my room with his registrar closely behind him for the day. I couldn't believe it. As Mr Schreuder spoke to me, my mind had escaped to reliving the hospital bed upstairs and the racing cars driving all over my body and reversing repeatedly over my head. The nausea returned and I just couldn't speak. Instead I thought, 'I *can't believe that you have Schumacher with you*'. I had clocked his name badge from a distance. That's not meant to be disrespectful or offensive to his registrar; after all I had never met him before. Mr Schreuder had always been oblivious to the hallucinations that I experienced and I certainly would have never told him how poorly they had made me, because the bottom line was, he had done his very best for me and I, of course, knew it. He is a unique consultant who cares about all of his patients and makes sure that his patients are aware of that too. The last thing I would have ever wanted to do at that time was tell him how poorly the surgery had made me feel.

But back to the job in hand he asked me if I had put the tiny plasters on. Needless to say, I was all marked up for theatre, and the nipples ended up in the perfect position with no thanks to my input.

I was so nervous about that procedure that I was allowed to have a little pre-med for the first time ever. A lovely little tablet that took all my worries and anxieties away. It was such a lovely feeling, being drowsy and being wheeled down to theatre instead of walking. It just completely took the edge away for me. I was incredibly relaxed in the anaesthetic room with the chirpy anaesthetist who had put me to sleep a number of times; I wish I had got his name. He kept talking to me and I really can't remember a thing about being put to sleep. Very civilised I felt, I'm definitely doing that next time if there ever has to be one.

My experience is the pre-med makes you drowsier when you come round from the operation. I was unable to wake up on the ward for hours afterwards. It was too much effort to engage with my friends when they came to visit me later in the afternoon. I bet they thought the hospital parking had been a waste of money! I actually quite liked the woozy, relaxed feeling of drifting off into a lovely peaceful sleep with the slight breeze blowing through the windows, faintly brushing over the surface of my skin. Unfortunately this was replaced by nausea by evening and I opted to stay in hospital overnight. I ended up having a really restless night sleep, probably due to having far too much sleep in the afternoon, coupled with the restlessness of the other patients in the bay with me. I had been spoilt previously needing to be in a room on my own so I wasn't that familiar with the sounds of the night ward. Although it did make a change in the early morning when we were all awake and could have a cup of tea and a little chat to help pass the time away. I felt so much better than the previous evening and didn't feel any discomfort following the surgery. I knew that I would be discharged following the ward round. I made sure that I got myself washed and dressed really early so I was ready to go home. It was the registrar that came round and checked me over and completed all the discharge forms. I had never met this registrar before the surgery. Registrars tend to move from one hospital to another quite frequently as part of their training process. As I started to say thank you for absolutely everything that had been done for me, I felt like it was falling on deaf ears. He didn't know me either. He hadn't seen his consultant and the rest of his team work so hard on me and come through everything together. I had already pieced together in my mind what I was going to say to Mr Schreuder for everything that he had done for me and starting to say it to his registrar meant absolutely nothing to me at all. As soon as he walked away and left me, the flood gates opened and the tears flowed and just didn't stop. Somehow I had managed to contain all of my feelings and emotions and now the end of the road was here, this was it. My surgery was now all complete and the very person that I really wanted to say thank you to wasn't there. Instead I sobbed uncontrollably and I'm sure the nurses on the ward thought that I was some sort of unstable character as they really didn't know me. I was on the day surgery ward. If I had been on the ward I was normally on after surgery I'm sure the nurses would have fully understood as they had cared for me so much. There was a nurse, however, who noticed my sudden outburst, as she drew the curtains around my bed for privacy. She tried to comfort me but I was inconsolable. She took it upon herself and telephoned Helen, Mr Schreuder's secretary, to come and see me. I fell to pieces in her arms. I couldn't believe it was all over. I had really needed and relied on these people around me to get me through it. They had done so in such an exceptional way, and now it was all over, the huge level of trust, the strong relationships built had now come to a natural close, and the biggest irony in everything that I have been through stabbed me through the heart, and totally flawed me. Some breast cancer survivors speak very freely over the sense of loss they feel when they lose their breasts and how it has a catastrophic effect on how they feel about their body - how unfeminine they feel. I won't ever dispute that. However, having immediate reconstructions meant I only ever felt that for the days following surgery. Once I recovered I never looked back. My biggest sense of loss had just hit me at great force. I was about to lose the very people who I had trusted with my life, whose support will always be unforgettable. They kept my mind alive at my most challenging period of life. I think of them in a really loving, admirable way and will continue to do so for the rest of my days. They were my best friends through my darkest days and now it was time to say goodbye. It doesn't matter how strong a person you are, emotions will always resurface at some point when you are least prepared. For me it was due to Mr Schreuder not being there to say *thank you*. It reduced me to a wreck. Poor Helen must have wondered what had happened to her on that morning. She was aware of my affections towards the department; we had almost been a little family taking the road together. Helen had always been on the other end of the phone at times of great anxiety just calming me down and taking my worries away. She was definitely instrumental in ensuring I returned to my happy and healthy self. I gave her a warm, affectionate cuddle, as Giles did, too, and we all wiped away our tears. I eventually managed to pull myself together and really expressed my appreciation for her being so kind to us.

That drive home was really strange. I can only compare the way that I felt to being homesick - for the hospital. I had faced so many fears towards it, I never realised how secure I felt within it. They are my inspiration in completing this book.

48

Freddie Phillips

With all the treatment over I needed to instil some routine and normality along with fun back into our lives. I had promised the girls a dog once all of the treatment was over. It would help us make a new start towards living a happy life as me move towards the future. We discussed this at great length and we all agreed, led by Annie, that we wanted to have a Shih Tzu, a small dog to have in the home with a lovely temperament around the children and a lap dog for me to sit and cuddle. Of course, we had the perfect name for it; we'd actually had the name for months and wanted to call it Fred, clearly named after Mr Schreuder and a really fantastic name for the breed. It seemed to take us ages to find a breeder, until one Sunday morning when the free local newspaper came through the door and in the pets for sale section were Shih Tzu puppies. We didn't hesitate to phone and enquire about them. There were still three for sale and we drove out in the afternoon to have a look at them. The breeder was only half an hour's drive from us. As soon as the four of us saw those tiny balls of fluff we couldn't resist them. The only problem was, there were not any little boys for sale. Just a little girl with the tip off her tongue hanging out, her big round eyes staring up at us was looking rather dumb. "We won't be able to call it Fred" Annie sniffed.

"Oh well, it doesn't matter - we can call her Freddie instead, short for Fredericka" Giles said and laughed. Giles is destined never to have any male companions in the house after growing up with three sisters, and having two daughters. Even the cat and rabbit turned out to be girls. So Freddie was named and taken into our hearts for many reasons. Maybe we just were not supposed to have the little boy. Somehow walking through the fields calling "Fred, come here mummy's little boy" seems marginally disrespectful. Freddie is the perfect dog and a much needed walking companion for me and although only little she really doesn't object to ranking up the miles, just as long as she is with you she is content. Freddie is such a loving dog and although only small she thinks she is a huge dog in small dog's body. She really doesn't get fazed by any other dogs on her travels, happily putting them in their place when the need arises. What is quite hilarious, though, is the irony that she suffers from emotional separation disorder and had a phobia to scissors and clippers in the early days (not the best characteristics for one named after a surgeon). This resulted in her needing to have an anaesthetic each time she has her hair cut to prevent her from becoming too distressed, and this happened every six weeks. Thankfully, for Freddie and our bank balance, she has grown accustomed to her grooming routine.

49

Never look back as life returns to normal.

Iknow that I must remain positive for reasons of sanity if for nothing else. Breast cancer has inevitably changed my personal outlook on life and allowed me to make small changes to ensure my future is as healthy as possible. Experiences in life naturally mould the person you become. I could never remain as the person I was as I have learned so much. I do appreciate that I have clearly had my fair share of lucky escapes than most but my days are not over yet. I must have one special guardian angel looking out for me! It's an understatement to say that I value just living for today; just to be here and watch my family grow is all I will ask for in life. Material things are worthless and have no place in the whole scheme of life. It is your underlying strength and self determination to succeed that will get you through life.

Don't get me wrong, surviving cancer can also be tough. Outwardly it is very easy to portray positivity, but there are still days for no apparent reason, when I can be shocked by my reaction to cancer. My heart still sinks into the deepest pit of my stomach when I learn that someone

I know has been diagnosed, or when I read a newspaper article or simply listen to the news, when I discover that someone else has lost their battle with cancer. It always reminds me of what I have been through and I have to convince myself how lucky I am to have survived two rounds. I'm never going to be in total control of the future. Yes, common sense does prevail and I have made beneficial adjustments to my lifestyle in terms of healthy eating, taking regular physical activity, making time for relaxation and avoiding stress as much as humanly possible. I would love to say abstaining from alcohol too, but the occasional few glasses of wine have crept back into one of my many pleasures.

I'm sure by now the chances of recurrence are small, but you are never given the all clear. I don't think there is such a thing as the complete cure of cancer at this stage apart from in the media world. Even my farewell appointment with my oncologist left me with deep emotional thought. H*opefully* this will be the last time we meet in the best possible sense of the word, she said to me. I did ask her what my chance of recurrence was, but the very second I said it I knew that I really didn't want to know and told her so.

In the hospital system you are surrounded by professionals - experts who want the very best outcome for you, who are just so positive about your future. But you do leave that system and the security and the safety of that environment and before you know it you are back out into the big wide world where you suddenly become just a statistic. As a survivor I hate this, and this is where your strength of character and power of the mind, whatever your spiritual beliefs, are challenged. I will eventually rise above this and use my second diagnosis of cancer as an opportunity to continue to make little beneficial adjustments to my life and always to set myself personal goals. I want to simply value living for now. I'm sure that over the course of time this will all fade into the distance and my lesson learnt will be to never look back, or try and rewind my life because it is a life that has made me the person I am. I can never change it but what I can do is look forward with the greatest hope that the future will for now and, always be bright. If anyone ever came to me for advice and asked me if I ever regretted any decision I have made along the way I would hold my hands on my heart and say most definitely not. I don't know life without experiencing cancer and although I have experienced many fears along the way I wouldn't have allowed anything to be done any differently for me. Yes, every day when I look in the mirror I see scars on my body, but not scars that act as an unpleasant memory but instead scars that tell and exude a very personal story. If I had to look forward to just one thing in the future I would just ask for life to finally return to normal. To look forward to spending time with those closest to me and pray that my dreaded relationship with cancer does not enter my world again and threaten to attack me and take me from the people who need me the most, because if it ever did, it would be faced with an even stronger battle of the mind.

I am still an enthusiastic supporter of Breakthrough Breast Cancer as they continue to make strides into finding targeted treatments for triple negative breast cancer, the form of the disease that I am most interested in. Recently I was involved as the case study, in the first conference held in London, into this type of the disease and was fortunate to meet scientists from all over the world who came together to share their findings. Once more demonstrating how lucky I am to be a survivor of this aggressive form of the disease. I try to fulfil many fundraising opportunities on their behalf in the form of organising activities or events or simply standing in Sainsbury's holding collection tins for small donations. It is on these occasions that you realise again just how many people are affected by cancer, and those strangers are only willing to make a donation but sadly are tearful when they remember a loved one as they share those few words with you.

During breast cancer awareness month I proudly posed topless with my husband cupping my breasts along with a couple of other Breakthrough supporters to help raise the awareness. I personally treated that pose as a true celebration of everything that has been done for me and felt confident striking the pose with Giles by my side.

I believe in Breakthrough's mission – *to save lives through enabling and ensuring access to improvements in breast cancer prevention, diagnosis and treatment*, and also their vision – *a future free from the fear of breast cancer.*

Every patient who enters the hospital system for treatment has the right to receive the highest standard of care and expertise and most importantly to be treated with dignity and respect. In my experience my expectations were exceeded, and now my story is told. Over the last couple of years friends have repeatedly asked me if I have found writing cathartic. I've always dismissed that - stating that I have only ever been motivated to write in the hope of raising funds for the hospital trust and team that treated me and looked after me so well as a simple means of saying thank you. As I start to pencil my finishing lines I never in a million years thought I would feel as exhausted as I do. Perhaps it has been stored upstairs and I needed to write to finally draw the curtains on the past.

Now it is time to move forward I wonder if I would ever find the courage to conquer my fear of jumping out of an aeroplane for charity. Would that parachute have the same protective force over me as my medical team and bring me back down to earth safely? Maybe one day I might find out and do it for Breakthrough.

Jack Trevor Story, the writer who defined the mania of carefree, easy credit living in his book "*Live Now Pay Later*," once wrote that "ordinary living takes ordinary nerve.' For some of us ordinary living suddenly takes extraordinary nerve. But it's amazing how many of us have it when faced with adversity. We've paid up front. It's time to live positively. We have a lot to teach those who take life for granted.

Acknowledgements and thanks.

I've often wondered what it must be like to make an Oscar speech or a speech following any award - this is the nearest I'm ever going to get to that. I'm really lucky to have my life blessed with so many friends, family and acquaintances that I cherish and feel worthy of mentioning now, just as my little tribute to you all so you buy the book. Firstly, thank you to Giles for all your love, support and humour along the way. It was the best tonic needed and just what the doctor ordered for me. Not only my great, supportive husband, but my best friend - my footprints in the sand - you certainly carried me through and showed me the way. Thankfully for you I have finished shouting across the lounge, "G - come and read this, or how do I spell..." To Olivia Jane and Annabel Louise, I'm so proud to be your mummy and I will never forget the loving way in which you looked after me at such tender ages - you made everything worth fighting for and I love you both with all of my heart and will always be here for you. To Mum and Dad, for all your love, support and guidance through life and for teaching me that you can achieve whatever you set out to do in life if you remain positive, focused and believe in yourself. Who would have ever thought I could write a book - but then I must have got the genes from somewhere! Oh well, at least I did inherit good genes as well! To Richard, for putting up with me and for being there, I couldn't ask for a better brother. To Lianne, you were my best friend through every single day. Our time together through my journey will always remain special to me. You found the right words at exactly the right moment so easily. I wish you still lived next door - you could have helped me with my writing, whilst I made the coffee! Please don't sue me for saying that! To Kathy, for our special friendship, I could always rely on you. Thanks for sitting beside me for hours on end when I needed you – I hate to think how many family size bars of Galaxy chocolate we, (I), consumed on all your visits. I'm sorry you live so far away from me now as our friendship took on a new dimension and you made me realise what it means to have a real friend. To Sarah, Joan, Helen, Jenny, Kathryn, Sheila, thank you for being wonderful friends through the decades and for giving me some great memories and years of laughter. To Jenny V, we've both had to jump huge hurdles in our way, but I think that we can hold our heads up high with dignity in how we have conducted ourselves in adversity – I know we are stronger people for coping with what life has kindly dealt us, and it's been more than most, but hey look at us – we're a force to be reckoned with. To Grandma for helping to look after the girls after school and keeping them entertained. To Deborah for stepping in and taking great care of Olivia and Annabel at short notice and for memorably shaving my head and making me look beautiful, for getting down on your hands and knees and scrubbing my wooden floor – now that is an image that will remain with me forever, or should I say with Giles forever! To all the staff at the Lower School, for retaining a safe, and secure environment for my girls, and for looking after them so well. You played an immense role in allowing them to come through the experience unaffected. To Jan and Mike, for all your help in supporting my fundraising efforts - you certainly did achieve the Ritz, with the help of many of the local ladies. I think Silsoe is a serious contender for the Great British Bake Off – all cakes looked amazing. Your support on the streets of London whilst I ran the marathon meant the world to me - but then I'd say anything to get a lift home! To Laura, for your kindness and thoughtfulness - you stepped in at the drop of a hat with any help I needed with fundraising, coupled with running a fantastic T-shirt and printing business. Thank you for all the T-shirts you donated to mark my events. To Robbie, for rising to the challenge and being the pivotal auctioneer, we certainly would not have raised the level of funds without your charisma. To friends who came into my life later on and everyone locally who has shown huge consideration towards me and offered support. I valued your kindness and welcomed your friendship. To the amazing friends who have supported my Worms on Parachutes page on Facebook, thank you for commenting or sharing my posts. To the carefully selected few I felt comfortable sharing Worms on Parachutes with – Laura, Bev, Tony, Richard, Wendy, Aurora and Dad, without your feedback I would never have the confidence to pursue it further. I was born with determination; self confidence seemed to escape me. To Richard Amos, who would have thought at twelve years old when I fixed your bicycle chain (because you didn't want to get your hands dirty) in Newport, you would be the *one* writing my foreword. I am extremely honoured you agreed to write it and I am exceptionally proud of everything that you have achieved in your professional life. Thank you for believing in me wholeheartedly. To my breast surgeon, breast care nurse, The Primrose Unit and all the special chemo nurses at Bedford Hospital, thank you for keeping my spirits high – you'll never be forgotten. To Ward 11B at Lister Hospital and all the nursing staff who looked after me so well, each and every one of you is a credit to the NHS. To Lesley the clinic nurse, thank you for being on hand in my many hours of need. To Amir, thank you for your care. If the NHS ever invent a role for someone to sit on all the patients beds and cheer them up, I would vote for you, your enthusiasm was infectious. To everyone who appeared in theatre unknown to me, thank you for your time. To Mr J, I did appreciate everything you did for me. Helen, so much more than a PA, thank you for everything and making me feel special and becoming a friend. And finally, to Fred, thank you for understanding me every step of the way. Thank you for taking great pride in everything you do and for never giving up. You gave me a great pair of breasts and the inspiration to write – you are on reflection that huge parachute!

3127205R00123

Printed in Great Britain
by Amazon.co.uk, Ltd.,
Marston Gate.